Weren't No
Good Times

Other Titles in the Real Voices, Real History Series™

My Folks Don't Want Me to Talk About Slavery,
Personal Accounts of Slavery in North Carolina
edited by Belinda Hurmence

Before Freedom, When I Just Can Remember,
Personal Accounts of Slavery in South Carolina
edited by Belinda Hurmence

We Lived in a Little Cabin in the Yard,
Personal Accounts of Slavery in Virginia
edited by Belinda Hurmence

On Jordan's Stormy Banks,
Personal Accounts of Slavery in Georgia
edited by Andrew Waters

Mighty Rough Times,
Personal Accounts of Slavery in Tennessee
edited by Andrea Sutcliffe

Prayin' to Be Set Free,
Personal Accounts of Slavery in Mississippi
edited by Andrew Waters

I Was Born in Slavery,
Personal Accounts of Slavery in Texas
edited by Andrew Waters

Cherokee Voices,
Early Accounts of Cherokee Life in the East
edited by Vicki Rozema

Voices from the Trail of Tears
edited by Vicki Rozema

John F. Blair, Publisher
WINSTON-SALEM, NORTH CAROLINA

Weren't No Good Times

Personal Accounts of Slavery in Alabama

EDITED BY
HORACE RANDALL WILLIAMS

Published by John F. Blair, Publisher

The paper in this book meets the guidelines
for permanence and durability of the
Committee on Production Guidelines for
Book Longevity of the Council on Library Resources.

Cover Image
Old Negro, near Camden, Alabama / Photographed by Marion Post Wolcott
Courtesy of The Library of Congress, Prints & Photographs Division,
FSA-OWI Collection 1935–1945, LC-USF33-030350-M5 DLC

Library of Congress Cataloging-in-Publication Data
Weren't no good times : personal accounts of slavery in Alabama /
edited by Horace Randall Williams.
p.   cm.   — (Real voices, real history series)
ISBN 0-89587-284-6 (alk. paper)
1. Slaves—Alabama—Biography. 2. Slaves—North Carolina—Social
conditions—19th century. 3. African Americans—Alabama—Interviews. 4. African Americans—Alabama—Social conditions—19th
century. 5. Alabama—Biography. I.
Williams, Randall, 1951–II. Series.
E445.A3W47 2004

306.3'62'0922761—dc22   2003023143

Design by Debra Long Hampton

Contents

Acknowledgments

Like almost everything that happens at NewSouth Books, where I work, the editing of these slave narratives turned out to be a team project. An exceptionally capable high school intern, Thomson McCorkle, initially located and secured copies of the narratives from the Library of Congress. Thomson also helped with research at the Alabama Department of Archives and History, where the staff was, as usual, accommodating and expert. Other NewSouth staff who helped with transcribing and typing included Pat Steele; interns Jenna Leith, Kathryn Moon, and Adrienne

Carter; and Foster Dickson, who also made helpful editing suggestions. My greatest help came from my ever-perceptive partner, Suzanne La Rosa, NewSouth's publisher, who did the preliminary editing on a good number of the narratives, reviewed the entire manuscript, helped with the final selections, and edited and shaped the introduction.

I am also grateful to the John F. Blair staff, especially Carolyn Sakowski, Anne Waters, Ed Southern, and Debbie Hampton. These long-time colleagues make the publishing process look far easier than it actually is. They, of course, also get the credit for having seen the value to begin with in making the slave narratives more accessible through this series.

Finally, this volume is dedicated to John Hope Franklin, about whom I wish to say a further word. Though we have met a couple of times, Dr. Franklin is not a close friend and I have never been his student, so the dedication is not of a personal nature. However, we have many mutual acquaintances within the ranks of Southern historians and I know the esteem and affection they have for him. I have admired his work since I first discovered it as an undergraduate thirty years ago. The influence of his body of work on the understanding of the history of slavery in America is justification enough for the dedication. But there is more.

It seems hard to believe, since he is still with us, but it was in the early 20th century when Dr. Franklin made his first Southern tour researching slavery records. One of the stops on that tour was at the Alabama Department of Archives and History, a few blocks from my office. Dr. Franklin tells stories about his early Southern research experiences in the context of the difficulty then for blacks coming into the South and trying to figure out the rules of segregation, because the rules were always variable, whether one was in a BBQ joint or a state history archives. In North Carolina, the white archives staff had refused to pull his research requests from the stacks, which led white researchers to complain that Franklin was getting unfair access by being "allowed" to pull his own records. In Alabama, he arrived at the archives and saw no signs or instructions, so he registered and then took a seat at a vacant table. An archives staffer then came bustling up and told him he shouldn't sit there, causing him to dread the coming ordeal. However, he was pleasantly surprised when the staffer continued, in a helpful tone, "Sit over here instead, this is a better place for you to work."

Later in his Alabama research, he needed some records that were restricted, which required a visit to the then-director, the formidable Marie Bankhead Owen. During their eventful first meeting she asked if he had met the "Harvard nigger" who was also doing research in the archives. Of course, he was the "Harvard nigger." Notwithstanding this rocky beginning, the young black man and the older white woman became friendly enough that she would invite him into her office for private conversations and exchanges of views. He has indicated that these visits gave him a unique perspective into old Alabama society.

I was mindful of this background when I visited the Alabama archives myself to look at perhaps some of the same documents Frankin had examined all those decades earlier. He was blazing the path in more ways than one.

Introduction

This is the seventh in John F. Blair's series of edited slave narratives begun in 1984 by Belinda Hurmence's *My Folks Don't Want Me to Talk About Slavery*. That first volume focused on North Carolina; subsequent volumes have covered Virginia, South Carolina, Georgia, Tennessee, Texas, and Mississippi. Now this one delves into Alabama, with additional slave states of the old Confederacy to follow.

The volumes all have as their beginning point the 1936–38 Federal Writers' Project (FWP) interviews with former slaves, most of whom were then in their eighties or nineties—a few even past the century mark. More than 2,000 former slaves in seventeen states were interviewed, resulting in about 10,000 pages of transcripts, which were then deposited with the Library of Congress.

The FWP was a part of the Works Progress Administration (WPA), a New Deal program intended to put people to work in ways that contributed to the nation. Some 6,600 writers, editors, and researchers worked on the project beginning in 1935. They earned only $20 to $25 a week, but jobs were so scarce during the Depression that most were probably glad for any work they could get. When federal funding expired in 1939, the project continued on a limited basis with state funding until 1943.

Some WPA projects built courthouses and schools, but the individuals involved in the FWP left a different legacy, a significant and wide-ranging exploration of the cultural fabric of the nation.

The effort was not universally admired. Some critics thought it was a waste of scarce resources during the bleak Depression years to spend money on intangibles such as art and literature. And Texas Congressman Martin Dies, Jr., a 1930s forerunner of the McCarthy era, believed the overall WPA (and the New Deal itself) was a communist plot.

Nonetheless, reports historian Douglas Brinkley, the FWP ultimately published more than 275 books, 700 pamphlets, and 340 articles, leaflets, and radio scripts. Brinkley notes that some of the most significant American literary figures of the twentieth century worked on the project, including John Cheever, Conrad Aiken, Nelson Algren, Saul Bellow, Arna Bontemps, Malcolm Cowley, Edward Dahlberg, Ralph Ellison, Zora Neale Hurston, Eudora Welty, Claude McKay, Kenneth Patchen, Philip Rahv, Kenneth Rexroth, Harold Rosenberg, Studs Terkel, Margaret Walker, Richard Wright, and Frank Yerby.

Alfred Kazin wrote that the FWP began with the mission of inventorying the hardships of the Great Depression but ended up "reporting on the national inheritance" in such a way that it changed the course of American literature.

Among the best-known of the FWP products is the collective *American Guide Series* of guidebooks to each of the states. Thousands of oral histories were also recorded by FWP interviewers. Many of the interviews are now available on the Library of Congress's WPA Life Histories Web- site: memory.loc.gov/ammem/wpaintro/wpahome.html. The interview subjects included poets, novelists, and artists, but also laborers, the homeless, and former slaves.

The richness of the narratives and the diversity of voices make the overall project a unique window into the American past. In the case of the ex-slaves—because few were literate enough to leave written accounts of their experiences—these interviews are often the only historical record of the thoughts and recollections of those who had been in bondage.

The interviews were compiled and deposited in the Library of Congress under the title *Slave Narratives: A Folk History of Slavery in the U.S. from Interviews with Former Slaves*. There they lay until 1972, when historian George Rawick edited and published a set of the narratives organized by state under the title *The American Slave: A Composite Autobiography*. This was followed by a Rawick-led project to uncover additional narratives that had for various reasons been omitted from the original Library of Congress collection. This ten-volume supplement to *The American Slave* was published in 1979.

As valuable as was the original collection, which was enhanced by the work of Rawick and his colleagues, the sheer volume of the material made it inaccessible to most potential readers. Belinda Hurmence, editor of the previously mentioned North Carolina, South Carolina, and Virginia volumes in the present Blair series, was one of the first editors to distill the material into smaller bites for average readers.

Andrew Waters, editor of the Mississippi, Georgia, and Texas entries in the series, retraced Hurmence's steps this way in his introduction to the Mississippi volume:

> Finding the collection of rough drafts, duplicate versions, and third-person accounts unnecessarily intimidating, she decided to pare it down to North Carolina narratives that would be more accessible to the general public. Her 1984 book, *My Folks Don't Want Me to Talk about Slavery*, contained twenty-one narratives selected for their quality. Hurmence's criteria were that the narratives had to be first-person accounts and that they had to contain memories of life under slavery and recollections of the Civil War. The second criterion was necessary because many of those interviewed by the Federal Writers' Project were born just before the Civil War and had no clear memories of slavery. That first collection was followed by a similar South Carolina collection, *Before Freedom, When I Just Can Remember*, and a Virginia collection, *We Lived in a Little Cabin in the Yard*.
>
> This—like the other slave-narrative collections subsequently published in this series—adheres closely to Hurmence's successful formula. All of the narratives in *Prayin' to Be Set Free* are written in the first person, which captures these elderly Americans' human vital-

ity in a way that third-person accounts cannot. Each former slave provides an account of life under slavery, and the majority tell about their experiences during the Civil War.

... The major editorial challenge in this collection was the issue of dialect. Dialect was employed heavily by the writers and editors of the Federal Writers' Project, presumably because they felt it was as important to preserve the subjects' way of talking as it was to preserve what they said. Unfortunately, the heavy use of dialect can make the narratives challenging to modern readers. I suppose it would have been possible to correct all the unusual spellings and abbreviations, but that did not seem the ideal solution, since the manner of speaking is part of the stories. Therefore, I attempted to balance these two issues, correcting obscure abbreviations and misspellings but leaving the unusual syntax intact. Obscure words are often interpreted within brackets, and editorial notes are employed to clarify confusing accounts. Many of these devices were added by the original interviewers and editors. I have also added my own when I felt it was necessary.

And so it has been with this volume, although I may have gone further than Waters in leaving in some of the dialect as reproduced by the original FWP interviewers; Waters himself had gone further than Hurmence, who seems to have cleaned up her narrators' language more than I felt comfortable doing. I felt that the slight added difficulty of the dialect was more than compensated for by hearing the voices as nearly as possible to how they apparently spoke to their interviewers in the 1930s.

I was guided to this approach by the example of Ruby Pickens Tartt, who conducted some of the best of the Alabama narratives. In fact, it was an edifying and humbling experience as a writer-editor to come along sixty-five years later and see the sparkle in her interviews compared to the flatness of some of the other FWP interviews, which are so slight as to be not useful. Tartt can be fairly described as the mother of folklore in Alabama. In addition to her work with the FWP, she collected folktales, folk songs, children's games and rhymes, and left a rich body of work that has been widely used by all the Alabama folklorists and historians who have followed her through the decades.

Tartt had an exceptional ear for language and speech, and I trusted her recording of her subjects' dialect. When she wrote *sot* for *sit/set* or *hyared* for *heared* I had no doubt that the ninety-one-year-old George Young said the words that way, or that he used *heared* where a more educated speaker would have said *heard*. Also, I grew up in rural Alabama in a county that had been a vital part of the cotton culture. At age fifty-two, I am among the last of Alabamians—black or white—who have memories of picking cotton by hand not for a few minutes to see how it felt but because I needed the few dollars I would get for a day's hard labor under a hot sun. The cadences and words I read in these ex-slave narratives from the 1930s were not that far removed from what I had heard as a boy and a young man in those cotton fields and on Saturdays in the shops and on the streets of the small town that was my county seat. So I may have left more dialect in my edited interviews than some of the previous editors in this series would have. However, I did substitute *these* for *dese*, *they* for *dey*, *the* for *de*, and so forth, because the interviews were so full of these bits of dialect that I felt to leave them in unnecessarily slowed reading. I also tried to minimize the use of apostrophes to indicate elisions such as *'em* for *them* or *'bout* for *about*. To do so, I chose the simple technique of simply writing *bout*, *em*, and *jes* in instances where I felt the reader would have no difficulty.

The next editorial issue was that of selectivity. There were 125 interviews identified with Alabama in the archives at the Library of Congress. The ex-slave interviews in general are uneven in quality and each of the editors of the John F. Blair series has had to wrestle with this difficulty. As Belinda Hurmence pointed out in the introduction to her first volume, the FWP interviewers were "supplied with a list of questions to ask, told to write down the answers as nearly verbatim as possible, and by and large that is what they did. The result is a remarkably eloquent prose."

But not always. Some of the interviewers, like Tartt, were quite skillful in their questioning and in the organization and editing of their material. The interviews that work the best are those where the former slave is allowed to speak and the interviewer's presence is almost invisible except in the occasional instance where the subjects directly address the "white folks" interrogating them. In such cases you get passages like Anthony Abercrombie describing his encounter with a "haint": "By dat time my houn' dog was crouching at my feets, wid de hair standin' up on his back and I couldn't make him git up or budge." Unfortunately, some of the interviews could not be included in a collection of first-person stories, because the interviewers simply paraphrased what they were told, as in, "Uncle Charlie said he drove many a load of cotton in the large mule wagons."

Another batch of the Alabama narratives had to be omitted because the former slaves were too young at the end of the Civil War to have any firsthand recollections of the war or of slavery. I also omitted those narratives where the interviews were conducted in Alabama but the former slave had moved to Alabama after Emancipation and thus his or her experiences of slavery were in another state.

Finally, I added one narrative, the last in this volume, which is not from the FWP material and is not actually an interview. The account of Louis Hughes of his experiences as a slave hired out by his master to work in a Confederate salt works is from Hughes's autobiography, *Thirty Years a Slave*, written and published by himself in 1897 after he had become a successful businessman in Milwaukee, Wisconsin. [This book was republished in 2003 by NewSouth Books, with an introduction by William L. Andrews.] I included the Hughes material because it is exceptionally eloquent and because it reflects a perspective largely missing from the FWP material, that of well-spoken, articulate, educated former slaves who were speaking for themselves and not weighing what they were saying by the effect it might have on a white stranger. The late historian C. Vann Woodward commented that "the most serious sources of distortion in the FWP narratives came not from the interviewees but from the interviewers—their biases, procedures, and methods—and the interracial circumstances of the interviews." Thus, while some of the interviewees are extremely candid, one hears in many of the narratives hints of reticence that could come from fear, nostalgia, politeness, or any number of other reasons.

Andrea Sutcliffe, editor of the Tennessee volume of the series, addressed the issue of interviewer-induced bias in the introduction to *Mighty Rough Times, I Tell You*. She explained that only twenty-six FWP interviews were included in the Library of Congress collection for Tennessee and that part of the reason may be that the Social Sciences Department at Fisk University, the distinguished black institution in Nashville, had already conducted a large number of such interviews in 1929–30. Sutcliffe writes,

> Readers who are familiar with WPA slave narratives from other states may notice a distinct difference in both the tone and content of many of the accounts in this collection. In particular, the interviewees in the Fisk University project were more outspoken, on the whole, than the WPA subjects about the cruelties they endured under slavery. One possible reason is that the Fisk interviews were conducted by Ophelia Settle Egypt, a Howard University graduate who was working for Dr. Charles Johnson, a professor in Fisk's Social Sciences Department. Both were black, and it is possible that the former slaves felt comfortable relating their experiences to a black professional woman who encouraged them to speak about their experiences, good and bad. By contrast, many of the WPA interviewers were white women from

the middle and upper classes in the communities where the interviews were conducted. No doubt many had ties to local charitable and governmental organizations that Depression-era blacks relied on for help.

Sutcliffe also points out that Rawick, in the introduction to *The American Slave*, documents censorship on the part of some of the state project directors of narratives that were "too hot" and either not forwarded to the central office in Washington or were "toned down" first. One suspects that both factors could have been at work in the Alabama project.

Then we come to slavery itself. The topic is difficult for modern readers because it is painful and, in the South at least, remains political. Approaching a century and a half after slavery's end, its legacy is mostly unacknowledged but is reflected everywhere in contemporary Southern life. While Alabama of the twenty-first century is a world apart from the darkest days of slavery and the dark days of segregation—the state now has more elected black officials than any other, to cite just one example—there is no escaping that the issues of race persist at both individual and institutional levels.

Although individual Alabama blacks now live and shop wherever they can afford and are welcome in all but a few mossback country clubs and mystic societies, it is also true that blacks still trail behind whites in almost all the state's demographic indicators, from incarceration rates to infant mortality, from average income to high school graduation rates, from home ownership to employment, etc. One has to be particularly hardheaded to look at the dismal educational performance of the public schools in majority black rural Alabama counties and not see a historical correlation with fact one, that it was illegal in Alabama for masters to educate their slaves; and fact two, that in the century after Emancipation the state's per pupil expenditures for educating blacks were a small fraction of what was spent per pupil for educating whites.

As well, Alabamians' views of slavery are skewed because prior to 1970 the textbooks used in both black and white schools taught the myth of happy slaves and kind masters, while too many history professors in the state's colleges still rhapsodized about states' rights and the Lost Cause. This background of miseducation and noneducation means that most Alabama citizens happily go about their daily lives hardly ever thinking about slavery, but when they do their views must be filtered through conflicting myths and stereotypes.

And today there is the added wrinkle of white guilt on the one hand and on the other white backlash against such issues as affirmative action, continued federal judicial oversight of local elections, and, more recently, the growing push for reparations.

The FWP interviews go a long way toward clearing up some of these misunderstandings because the former slaves' powerful voices are offering direct testimonies about what they saw and experienced.

Alabama was a frontier state, and from the beginning its economy was built on cotton and slavery and its laws were fashioned to accommodate both. As Native Americans—the Creeks, Choctaws, Cherokees, and Chickasaws—were driven from the state, land speculators and cotton farmers poured in. Some of the wealthiest of these new Alabamians were abandoning played-out plantations in Virginia, the Carolinas, and, to a lesser extent, Georgia. They brought with them large numbers of slaves to begin exploiting the fertile acreage in Alabama's Black Belt (so named for its rich, dark soil) and in the Tennessee River valley. In 1820, a year after statehood, the slave population in Alabama was 41,879, as compared to 85,451 whites and 571 free blacks. By 1850, there were 342,884 slaves, 426,514 whites, and 2,265 free blacks. By 1860, the numbers were 435,080; 526,271; and 2,690. The expansion of Alabama's cotton trade had thus swelled the slave numbers from about a third of the total population in 1820 to nearly half in 1860.

Some of the increase came about through what amounted to breeding of slaves, with slave women being rewarded for delivery of healthy babies. The rest of the increase was from a profitable slave trade that imported "stock" from other states and from Africa (Congress had banned the international slave trade in 1808, but occasional slave ships still arrived in the port of Mobile up to the eve of the Civil War). John Smith of Uniontown told his interviewer that he was taken from his parents in North Carolina at age thirteen by slave-trading speculators, who "would feed em up and git em fat and slick and make money on em."

Much of Alabama's pre-Civil War wealth was tied up in its human capital. Historian Leah Atkins reports that by 1860, "good field hands in Alabama peaked at $1,600, while a skilled slave might bring twice that amount." Thus, Alabama slaveowners lost an estimated $200 million of capital to Emancipation.

In recent years, Atkins and her fellow Alabama historians, often following in the footsteps of John Hope Franklin's groundbreaking *From Slavery to Freedom: A History of Negro Americans*, have published texts which draw from the narratives to dispel some of the myths about slavery. For instance, while there were Black Belt planters who owned hundreds of slaves, Atkins reports that slave property was no less important for yeoman farmers and poorer whites in the hill country and gives as an example a Jefferson County man whose entire estate was probated in 1824 at $1,896, of which all but $70 was in the value of a slave couple and four children. The records also show that slaves were owned in Alabama by Indians and free blacks (Angie Garrett of Livingston describes in her interview the poignant story of a free black entrepreneur who ran into financial difficulties and sold his own children).

Another prevalent myth was that because slaves were so valuable, masters could not afford to mistreat them and therefore the stories of cruel treatment were simply abolitionist propaganda. However, the historian J. Mills Thornton, author of *Politics and Power in a Slave Society: Alabama 1800–1860*, reports that as Southern fears of abolition increased, callous punishment of slaves became more common. Thornton writes that on two occasions, in 1854 and 1856, the citizens of Mount Meigs, a "wealthy and relatively cultured planting community" near Montgomery, gathered to watch accused slaves being burned alive. "The spectators listened to the screams of the tortured victims with all the impassivity of Aztec priests, observing sacrifices to gods equally as bloody and as terrible as the Furies who ruled the heart of the South."

Martha Bradley of Mount Meigs was probably referring to one of these incidents when she told her interviewer, "Well, when they got him they found out what he'd done and was gwine to burn him alive. Judge Clements, the man that keep law and order, say he wouldn't burn a dog alive, so he left. But they sho' burn that nigger alive for I seed him after he was burned up."

The inherent cruelty and violence of the "peculiar institution" is unavoidable in the testimonies of the former slaves. The horrors to both slave and master are chillingly evident in the scene described by Amy Chapman of Livingston of a slave who was beaten almost to death and later, having waited for an opportunity for revenge, plunged her tormentor's baby into a washpot of boiling lye, killing the child.

In this context, one reads with interest the remarks of James Redpath, a British-born abolitionist journalist for Horace Greeley's *New York Tribune*, who secretly interviewed a number of slaves during three trips he made through the South in the 1850s. His writings have been collected and annotated in *The Roving Editor, or Talks with Slaves in the Southern States* by James Redpath, edited by

John R. McKivigan. Redpath was in Alabama in late 1854. He wrote:

> I have spoken with hundreds of slaves in Alabama, but never yet met one contented with his position under the "peculiar" constitutions of the South. But neither have I met with many slaves who are actively discontented with involuntary servitude. Their discontent is passive only. They neither hope, nor grumble, nor threaten. I have never advised a single slave either in Georgia or Alabama to run away. . . . The distance is too far; the opportunities and the chance of escape too few. The slaves, I found, regard themselves as the victims of a system of injustice from which the only earthly hope of escape is—the grave!

Redpath's observations are mirrored in the Alabama slave narratives in this volume. A wide range of experiences is reported, from the benign view of slavery reported by Tildy Collins—"Old Marster was good to all he niggers"—to the sinister implications of Amy Chapman's recollection that there was "another mean man who was always a-beating nigger women cause they wouldn't mind him."

Thus, the FWP slave narratives help us as readers to understand that slavery had varying truths: the institution was evil and it corrupted everything it touched, yet within the evil institution there could be relationships between slaves and masters that were humane and respectful—as long as, of course, it suited the master.

And the narratives lead us ultimately to lament with

George Young of Livingston: "Miss, whar was the Lord in them days? Whut was He doin'?"

Weren't No
Good Times

I Ain't Never Been a Slave

Nicey Pugh
PRICHARD

I was bawn a slave, but I ain't never been a slave. There was eleven chilluns in my family and all em are dead cepting me and one brother, who is seventy-five year old at the present time. My pappy's name was Hamp West, and my mammy was Sarah West. All my folks belonged to Massa Jim Bettis and was bawn and raised on his place.

When I was a little pickaninny I worked in Massa Jim's house, sweepin' and a-cleanin'. Us slaves had to be up at the house by sun-up, build the fires, and git the cookin' started. They had big open fireplaces with pot racks to hang the pot on. That's whar us boiled the vegetables. And, honey, us sho' had plenty somep'n t'eat: greens, taters, ros'nears [roasting ears of corn], and plenty of home-killed meat. Sometimes my oldest brother, Joe West, and Friday Davis, another nigger, went huntin' at night and kotched mo' possums than we could eat. They'd ketch lots of fish; enough to last us three days.

I 'members one day when me and another nigger gal were a-going after the cows in the field and us seed what I reckon was the Ku Klux Klan. Us was so skeered we didn't know whut to do. One of them walked up to us and say: "Niggers, whar you goin'?"

"Us is just after the cows, Mr. Ku Klux," us said. "Us ain't up to no devilment."

"All right, then," they say. "Just you be sho' that you don't git to none."

After we got home us told the massa about the 'sperience, and he jes laugh. He tol' us that we warn't goin' to be hurt iffen we was good; he say that it was only the bad niggers that was goin' to be got after by them Ku Klux.

When we was little we didn't have no games to play, cause Massa Jim and Miss Marfa didn't have no chilluns, and I ain't never had no 'speriences with haints or hoodoos. They never teach us to read or write cause when the niggers learn anything, they would git uppity and want to run away. We would have Sat'day afternoons off, then us would sweep the yards, and set around on benches and talk. It was on the benches that most of us slaves set in warm weather. We et outen tin cups and us used iron spoons to shovel the food in.

At Christmastime, Massa would have a bunch of niggers to kill a hog and barbecue him, and the womens would make 'lasses cake, and Old Massa Jim had some kinda seed that he made beer outen, and we-alls drank beer round Christmas.

But there warn't no other time like New Year's. Us all celebrated in a big way then. Most of them no 'count niggers stayed drunk for three days.

And as for the funerals, I don't ever 'member but three white folks dyin'. They jes didn't seem to die in them days, and the ones that did die was mostly kilt by somep'n. One white gentleman got hisself kilt in a gin 'chinery and another was kilt workin' on the big road.

Then there was a white woman who was kilt by a nigger boy cause she beat him for siccin' a dog on a fine milk cow. He was the meanest nigger boy I ever seed. I'll never forgits the way them white mens treated him after he had his trial. They drug him through the town behin' a hoss, and made him walk over sharp stones with his bare feets, that bled lak somebody done cut em with a knife. They never give him no water all that day and kept him out in the boilin' sun 'til they got ready to hang him. When they got ready to hang him, they put him up on a stand and chunked rocks at his naked body; they threw gravel at his eyes and broke his ribs with big rocks. Then they put a rope around his neck and strung him up 'til his eyes popped outen his head. I knew it was a blessin' to him to die.

But all and all, white folks, them was really happy days for us niggers. Course we didn't have the 'vantages that we has now, but there was somep'n back there that we ain't got now, and that's security. Yassuh, we had somebody to go to when we was in trouble. We had a massa that would fight for us, and help us, and laugh with us, and cry with us. We had a mistress that would nurse us when we was sick, and comfort us when we hadta be punished. I sometimes wish I could be back on the old place. I kin see the cool-house now packed with fresh butter, and milk, and cream. I kin see the spring down amongst the willows and the water a-trickling down between little rocks. I kin hear the turkeys a-gobblin' in the yard, and the chickens a-runnin' around in the sun, and shufflin' in the dust. I kin see the bend in the creek just below our house, and the cows as they come to drink in the shallow water and gits their feets cool.

Yassuh, white folks, you ain't never seed nothing lak it so you can't tell the joy you git from lookin' for dewberries and a-huntin' guinea pigs, and settin' in the shade of a peach tree, reachin' up and pullin' off a ripe peach and eating it slow. You ain't never seed your people gathered bout and singin' in the moonlight, or heered the lark at the break of day. You ain't never walked acrost a frosty field in the early mornin', and gone to the Big House to build a fire for your mistress, and when she wakes up slow to have her say to you, "Well, how's my little nigger today?"

Nawsuh, just like I told you at first, I was bawn a slave but I ain't never been one. I's been a worker for good peoples. You wouldn't call that being a slave, would you, white folks?

Old Joe
Can Keep His Two Bits

Anthony Abercrombie
PERRY COUNTY

I always is been puny, but I reckon I does purty well considerin' I is a hundred years old. I knows I's that old cause my mistress put it down in the Bible. I was born on the fourth day, and I was a full-growed man when the war come on in '61.

I ain't seed none outen one of my eyes in near bout sixty years, and the doctor say I got a catalac [cataract] on the other one, but I knows you is white folks. Yassum, my mind kinder comes and goes, but can always 'member bout slavery time. Hit's the things what happen in these days that's so easy for me to disremember.

I belonged to Marster Jim Abercrombie. His plantation was bout sixteen miles north of Marion in Bibb County. He didn't care much bout me cause I was puny and warn't much 'count in the field. When young Jim married, Old Marse Jim gave me to him, and he fotched me to Perry County.

Old Marster didn't go to war cause he was corrupted; he was deaf in both ears and couldn't see good, neither.

My mistress, Miss Lou, was raisin' me up to be a carriage driver, and she was jes as good to me as she could be. She useta dose me up with castor oil, jimson root, and dogwood tea when I'd be feelin' po'ly, and she'd always take up for me when Marse Jim get in behind me bout somep'n. I reckon though I was a purty worrisome nigger in them days; always gettin' in some kind of mischief.

I useta go to meetin'. Us niggers didn't have no meetin' house on the plantation, but Marse Jim 'lowed us to build a bresh [brush] arbor. Then two years after the Surrender I took consideration and j'ined up with the Lord. That's how come I live so long. The Lawd done told me, "Antn'y, you got a hundred and twenty miles to trabel. That mean you gwine to live a hundred and twenty years, if you stay on the straight and narrow road. But if you don't, you gotter go jes the same as all the others."

Marse Jim had bout three hundred slaves, and he had one mighty bad overseer. But he got killed down on the bank of the creek one night. They never did find out who killed him, but Marse Jim always believed the field hands done it. 'Fore that us niggers useta go down to the creek to wash ourselves, but after the overseer got killed dar, us just leave off that washin', cause some of em seed the overseer's ha'nt down there floatin' over the creek.

Dar was another ha'nt on the plantation, too. Marse Jim had some trouble with a big double-j'inted nigger named Joe. One day he turn on Marse Jim with a fence rail, and Marse Jim had to pull his gun and kill him. Well, that happen in a skirt of woods where I get my lightwood what I use to start a fire. One day I went to them same woods to get some 'simmons. Another nigger went with me, and he clumb the tree to shake the 'simmons down whilst I be pickin' em up. 'Fore long I heared another tree shakin'. Every time us shake our tree, that other tree shake, too, and down come the 'simmons from it. I say to myself, "That's Joe, cause he likes 'simmons, too." Then I grab up my basket and holler to the boy in the tree, "Nigger, turn loose and drop down from dar, and ketch up with me if you can. I's leaving here right now, cause Old Joe is over dar gitting 'simmons, too."

Then another time I was in the woods choppin' lightwood. It was bout sundown, and every time my ax go whack on the lightwood knot, I hear another whack 'sides mine. I stops and listens and don't hear nothin'. When I starts choppin' ag'in I hears the other whacks. By that time my houn' dog was crouchin' at my feets, with the hair standin' up on his back, and I couldn't make him git up nor budge.

Dis time I didn' stop for nothin'. I jes drap my ax right dar, and me and that houn' dog tore out for home lickety-split. When us got dar Marse Jim was settin' on the porch and he say: "Nigger, you been up to somep'n you got no business. You is all outen breath. Who you runnin' from?"

Then I say: "Marse Jim, somebody 'sides me is choppin' in you woods, and I can't see him."

And Marse Jim, he say: "Ah, that ain't nobody but Ole Joe. Did he owe you anythin'?"

And I say: "Yassah, he owe me two-bits for helpin' him shuck corn."

"Well," Marse Jim say, "don't pay him no mind: it jes Ole Joe come back to pay you."

Anyhow, I didn't go back to them woods no mo'. Ole Joe can jes have them two-bits what he owe me, cause I don't want him follerin' round after me. When he do I can't keep my mind on my business.

Mules Be Eatin'
and Niggers Be Eatin'

Angie Garrett
GAINESVILLE

I was born in De Kalb, Mississippi. My mother was
Betty Scott, and I didn't know my father's name. I had
four brothers (Ember, Johnny, Jimmie, and Henry) and
three sisters (Delphie, Lizzie Sue, and Frankie), and my
grandmother was Sukie Scott. She lived five miles from
Gainesville across Noxubee Creek, and I lived with her.
Never axed bout my granddaddy, cause wasn't no tellin'.
My mammy lived right here in Gainesville and belonged
to Mr. Sam Harwood.

I belonged to the Moorings, and Cap'n Mooring run

on a boat to Mobile from Aberdeen, Mississippi, on the 'Bigbee River, and 'twas called the *Cremonia*. I was the house gal and nurse, and I slept on a pallet in Old Miss's room. I nursed the Moorings' little boy, Johnny. The little gal had died. I had a-plenty to eat long as us was on that boat, and hit sho was good.

But when us was in De Kalb, vittles was give out at the smokehouse—a slice o' meat, and piece of bread, and peas—and 'twas sarnt [sent] out ter the field. Mules be eatin', and niggers be eatin'.

Mr. Scott in De Kalb had bout fifty slaves, and a big plantation, and a overseer name of Barnes. He was a haughty man, and niggers was skeered to death cause he would come in a-cussin'.

Us would git up 'fore daylight. 'Twas dark when us go out, dark when us come in. Us make a little fire in the field some mawnins, hit be's so cold, and us let it go out 'fore the overseer come. If he seed you he'd make yer lay down flat on yo' belly, foots tied out and hands tied out, and whup you. The whup was a leather strap with a handle, a sho' Lawd slapper. I been whupped 'til I tell lies on myself to make em quit. Say they whup 'til I tell the truth, so I had to lie bout myself to keep em from killin' me.

This race is mo' like the chillun of Israel, cept they didn't have to shoot no gun ter set them free.

Sometimes us sing and have a little prayer meetin', but 'twas mighty easy and quiet-like. Gran'ma Sukie useta sing "Travel on, travel on, soon be over."

If any us died in them days, they buried us quick as

they could, and got out of dere, and got to work. At night they blow'd the horn for em to bring in the cotton what the women spinned. They made all the cloth. Us work at nights, too, but us rested Sundays. We didn't get no presents at Christmas. Sometimes us had a cornshuckin', and no celebration for no marriage. That was called "jumpin' the broom," jes taken up with em. They all want you to have plenty of chillun, though.

Us wore asfedity [asafetida] round us neck keep off the smallpox and measles. Us didn't have much medicine, and some of em was always full of bad complaints lak Carrie, my neighbor, what you axed about. I be's a-hurtin', but I can't never git in edgeways for her. Always got a lot excuses; don't never 'pects to die 'thout folks know what ails her. But she brought me some black-eyed peas today, and I laks em cause they biles [boils] soft, and I say if the devil brought hit, God sarnt [sent] hit. Sometimes I be's hongry, and I say, "Whut is I'm gwinter eat?," and along come somebody with somep'n.

Wish you could of heered that calliope on the *Cremonia*. They dance sometime 'most all night, but they didn't act lak they do now. 'Twas nice behaviour. Look lak ev'ything goin' back ter heathenism, and hit's on the way now. But the good Lord helps me. He hol's my hand. I ain't got nothin' 'gin nobody. I don't see no need of fussin', and fightin', and a-drinkin' whiskey. Us livin' in a new worl', and I go on making the bes' I kin of hit. Some I lak, some I don't.

I got one daughter, Fannie Watson, a good washer and ironer right here in Gainesville, and I got a son, too, say he ain't gonna marry 'til he kin treat the woman good as she can treat herself. I makes him wait on me, and he gits mighty raw sometimes, but I tells him I'm jes much older than he is now as I was when he was bawn. Then he gives me a old dirty dime, but now with these here tokens, you gotter pay some of hit fer spendin'. They tells me hit's the governor, and I say "Let him carry em; he kin tote em, I ain't able." Well, once ain't always, and twice ain't forever.

I don't never go ter church no mo'. The preachers here is goin' blind about money. They ain't interested in they soul. Some folks b'longs to the church and ain't been changed. The church ain't all of hit. I 'members day of 'mancipation. Yankees tole us we was free, and they call us up from the field to sign up and see if us wanted to stay on with em. I stayed that year with the Moorings, then I bargain for land, but couldn't never pay fer hit. Turned loose 'thout nothin.'

But they was a coal-black freeborn nigger named George Wright, had a floatin' mill right here on the 'Bigbee River, stayed at the point of the woods jes 'bove the spring branch, and hit did a good service. But he got in debt, and he sold his five boys. They was his own chillun, and he could sell em under the law. They names was Eber, Eli, Ezekiel, Enoch, and Ezra, and he sold em to the highes' bidder right yonder front of the post office for cash. And Jack Tom was another free nigger here and he bought some of em, and they others the white folks bought, and I never heerd no complaint, and I seed em as long as they lived.

They was a heap of things went on. Some I laks to

remember, some I don't. But I'd rather be free now. I never seed Mr. Lincoln. When they told me bout him, I thought he was partly God.

But Mr. John Rogers right here (he's dead and gone now), he was what he was and wasn't 'ceitful. Go to him if you got into anything, and he more'n apt to tell you what to do. He was wild when he was young, but he settle down and was the best white man to the niggers I ever knowed. He'd help me right now if he was livin' and seen me wearin' dis here rag nasty, he sho' would.

They Planted the
Silver in the Field

Georgia Mitchell

EUFAULA

I never seed my mammy. She died when I was bawn, and Mistress Mary Mitchell raised me in the Big House. I was named after her sister, Miss Georgia. I slep' in her room, and I was a house nigger all my days. I never went to a nigger chu'ch 'til I was grown and married. Didn' associate with niggers cause I was a nursemaid. I raised Miss Holly, her last baby.

I was bawn at "Elmoreland," Massa Americus Mitchell's place, mor'n ninety yeahs ago, and after Freedom I stayed there 'til Ole Massa died and my mistress moved to Eufaula to live with her son, Marse Harry.

Bout all I know of the war is when they said, "The Yankees is comin', the Yankees is comin'."

Us sho' was skeered, and there'd be some fast doin's about the place. All the cattle, and hawgs, and hosses we drive to the swamp on the nawth creek, and took the feather beds down there, too, and hid em in the bresh and leaves. My mistress tied her trinkets in sacks and put em in outlandish places lak the hen-house and the hayloft. And the silver, they planted in the field.

Escapes Whipping
by Pulling Frock Coattail

Frank Gill
MOBILE

I not only lived during slavery times, but I was here before a gun was fired, and before Lincoln was elected.

I was living in Vicksburg, Lee County, Mississippi, and my maw and paw's names was Amelia Williams and Hiram Gill. Mr. Arthur and George Foster owned us up 'til I was a big boy 'tween fourteen or fifteen years old. The way it was, their mother, Old Missy, was a widow and her had these two boys, and she had money. I tell you had barrels of money, so when the two boys got old enough she divided the slaves and property 'tween em. Me and my paw fell to Arthur Foster, and some of our kindred fell to George Foster. Mister George was a captain in the army and was killed near Vicksburg.

Old Missy's place sho' was big. I couldn't say how many acres there was, but it run four or five miles, and she owned hundreds of slaves. She had lots of log cabin quarters, what had the cracks daubed with mud, and then sealed with boards. I's telling you they was twice as warm as the houses we live in now. They had chimleys built of mud and sticks, and had big wide fireplaces that we cooked on, and the beds was homemade, but Lord, they was heaps stronger than they is now. Them boards was morticed together.

When I was on the old missy's place, I stayed around the house, and wait on them, and tend the horses. Another thing I had to do, they would send me for the mail. I had to go twelve miles after it, and I couldn't read or write, but I could bring everybody's mail to them jes right. I knowed I had better git it right. You see, I could kinda figure, so I could make out by the numbers.

Old Missy and Mr. Arthur both was good to me and all the slaves. They 'low the slaves to make their own patch of cotton, and raise chickens, and he would sell it for them. Cotton was the main crop in them days, it would sell as high as twenty-five cents a pound. Course they raises corn, pears, and other things on the plantation, too, but they made the cotton. Master Jesus! They sometimes made from fifty to one-hundred-and-fifty bales.

I 'members how all the women had looms, both black

and white, weaving cloth for the clothes; and they raised sheep to git the wool to make them gray uniforms. Lord, at sheep-shearing times it was big times. Them uniforms was made out of all wool, too, but I can't remember what they used to dye em gray, but I 'members they dyed with red oak bark, walnut bark, and also a brush what growed down on the branch. Also they used the laurel leaves to dye yellow, as well as clay. They sot the dye with salt, and it really stayed in.

They really fed us slaves good, up 'til such a length of time after the war broke out, then food began to git scarce.

You see, the government taxed em, and they had to give so much to feed the soldiers. Even then us had a good time. I 'members how the li'l chillun played ball and marbles, 'specially marbles, it was our big game. Even after night, they had a big light out in the backyard, and us would play. Sometimes us would hunt at night, and well I 'members one Saturday night I went hunting with my uncle, and didn't get in 'til daylight next mawning, and I was sleepy and didn't get the shoes all cleaned before church time. So Old Marster called me and took me to the carriage house to give me a whipping. Old Marster's boy was about the same age as me, and he beg his paw not to whip me, and I was begging, too, but he carried me on, and when we got in the carriage house, Old Marster had to climb up on the side wall to get the whip, and he had on one of those long-tailed coats, and it left them tails hanging down, so I jes grabbed hold of them, and made him fall, and then I run to the old missy's room, cause I knowed when I got in there that Old Marster would never hit me.

The old missy got up out of the bed and wouldn't let Old Marster whip me, and she got so mad that she told that she warn't going to church with him that morning, and that lak to kill the Old Marster, cause he sho' loved and was proud of Old Missy. She was a beautiful woman. That ended the whipping, and that's the only time I 'members him trying to whip me.

Old Missy didn't 'low em to whip the women either, and they wouldn't 'low the women to roll logs. But they did work them in the fields. Course they kept the young women with babies round the house, and they eat the same grub as the white folks eat.

Talking bout log rolling, them was great times, cause if some of the neighboring plantations wanted to get up a house, they would invite all the slaves, men and women, to come with their masters. The women would help with the cooking, and you may be sho' they had something to cook. They would kill a cow, or three or four hogs, and then have peas, cabbage, and everything like grows on the farm. And if there was any meat or food left they would give that to the slaves to take home, and jes before dark the overseer or Old Marster would give the slaves all the whiskey they wanted to drink. Sometimes after the day's work, they would have a frolic, such as dancing, and old-time games.

They would have these same kind of gatherings at corn-shucking time, and cotton-picking time, but there warn't so much foolishness at cotton-picking time, cause they didn't call one another then, cepting when the cotton got so far ahead of them, and it was bout to set in for a wet spell.

You asked me about the patterollers? You see the city policeman walking his beat? Well, that's the way the patterolling was, only each county had their own patterollers, and they had to serve three months at a time. And if they cotch you out without a pass, they would give you thirty-nine lashes, cause that was the law. The patterollers knew nearly all the slaves, and it wurn't very often they ever beat them.

You know folks were jes the same then as they is now, both black and white. Some folks you could neighbor with then, jes lak you can now, and there was good folks then, jes the same as they is now.

Christmastime was the best of all, cause us allus had a big dinner, and the old marster give the women calico dresses and shoes, and the men shoes and hats, and would give us flour, and sugar, molasses, and would buy beer, whiskey, and wine.

The old marster took good care of us, too. When any of us got sick he send for the doctor, then when they order the medicine to be given at night, he'd see that us got it. But nowadays if you get sick, you have to get the doctor, and then pay him yourself. Then the old marster had to find clothes and shoes for us, but now us has to scuffle and get them the best way us can.

You know, Miss, I's been here a long time. I even 'members Jefferson Davis. I've seen him many a time. He had a home between [Mobile] and New Orleans, and you knows he first took his seat in Montgomery and then moved to

Richmond, Virginny.

I 'members, too, how I used to think that the Baptist was the only religion. John the Baptist come here baptizing, and everybody had to offer up sacrifices, a goat or a sheep or somep'n, jes lak the man who was going to offer up his son for a sacrifice. But Jesus come and changed all that. The folks in them times didn't have nobody to worship, and then one come who said, "Father, hand me a body and I'll die for them." That's Christ, and he was baptized, and God give Jesus this whole world. So I believed that was the only religion.

I 'members how us would hold big baptizings and shout. Us allus went to church in the white folks' church; they had church in the mornings, us had ours in the afternoons. Us would have to have a pass, though, cause the church was eight miles away from the plantation.

There was plenty old songs us used to sing. There is this one that goes—

Wonderful Peter,
Wonderful Paul,
Wonderful Silas,
Who for to make-a
Mah heart rejoice.
Oh, Good Shepherds, feeda mah sheep.
Don't you hear the young lambs a-bleating?
Don't you hear the young lambs a-bleating?
Oh, Good Shepherds, feeda mah sheep.

Today's Folks
Don't Know Nothin'

Mary Ella Grandberry
SHEFFIELD

I'm some'eres nigh ninety years old. I was borned in Barton, Alabama. My father and mother come from Richmond, Virginny. My mammy was Margaret Keller, and my pappy was Adam Keller. My five sisters was Martha, Sarah, Harriet, Emma, and Rosanna, and my three brothers was Peter, Adam Jr., and William.

Us all live in a li'l two-room log cabin jes off the Big House. Life wasn't very much for us, cause we had to work and slave all the time. Massa Jim's house was a little old frame building lak a ordinary house is now. Massa Jim had one of the biggest plantations in that section, but jes to look at him you'd think he was a po' white man. There was no po' white trash in our community; they was kept back in the mountains.

I guess he had nigh onto a hundred blacks on the place. I never knowed zackly how many thar was nor how big the place was. There was a lot of cabins for the slaves, but they wasn't fitten for nobody to live in. We jes had to put up with em.

Massa Jim was a bachelor, and he ain't never had much truck with womenfolks. Iffen he had any chilluns, I never knowed nothing bout em.

I don't remember much about when I was a chile. I disremembers ever playing lak chilluns do today. Ever since I kin remember I had a water bucket on my arm toting water to the hands. Iffen I wasn't doing that, I was chopping cotton. Chilluns nowadays sees a good time to what we did then. Every morning jes about hip (the beginning)_ of day, the overseer was round to see that we was ready to git to the fields. Plenty times us had to go withouten breakfast, cause we didn't git up in time to git it 'fore the man done come to git us on the way to the field. Us worked 'til dinnertime jes the same before we got anything to eat.

The food we et was fix jes lak hit is now. My mammy fixed our grub at home. The only difference 'tween then and now was us didn't get nothing but common things then. Us didn't know what hit was to git biscuits for breakfast every morning. Hit was cornbread 'til on Sundays then us'd git four biscuits apiece. Us got fatback most every morning. Sometimes us might git a chicken for dinner on a Sunday or some day lak Christmas. Hit was mighty seldom us gits anything like that, though. We laked possoms and rabbits but they didn't come 'til wintertime when some of the men folks'd run cross one in the field. They never had no chance to git out and hunt none.

Us wore the same thing in summertime as in the wintertime. The same was true bout shoes. Us wore brogans from one year to another.

My old massa was a purty good man but nothin' extra. One thing bout him, he wouldn't allow none of the overseers to whup none of us, lessen he was there to see hit done. Good thing he was lak that, too, cause he saved the blacks many a lick what they'd got if he hadn't been there.

The overseers was terrible hard on us. They'd ride up and down the field and haste you 'til you near bout fell out. Sometimes and most generally ever time you behind the crowd you got a good licking with the bull whip that driver had in the saddle with him. I hear mammy say one day they whupped po' Leah 'til she fell out like she was dead. Then they rubbed salt and pepper on the blisters to make em burn real good. She so sore 'til she couldn't lay on her back nights.

Folks nowadays is always complaining bout how they is having such hard times, but they jes don't know nothing. They should have come up when I did and they see now they is living jes lak kings and queens. They don't have to git up 'fore day when hit's so dark you kin jes see your hand before your eyes. Hit was always good dark when the hands got in from the field. Course iffen there was a lady what had a baby at home, she could leave jes a little 'fore the sun set.

Younguns nowadays don't know what hit is to be pun-ished; they thank iffen they gits a little whupping from they mammy that they is punish terrible. They don't know what hit's lak to have to keep up with the leader. You know they was always somebody what could work faster than the rest of the folks and this fellow was always the leader, and everybody else was suppose to keep up. Iffen you didn't keep up with the leader you got a good thrashing when you gits home at night. They'd whup us iffen we was caught talking bout the free states, too. Iffen you wasn't whupped, you was put in the nigger box and fed cornbread what was made withouten salt and with plain water. The box was jes big 'nough for you to stand up in, but it had air holes to keep you from suffocating. There was plenty turning round room in hit to 'low you to change your position ever once in a while. Iffen you had done a big enough thang you was kept in the nigger box for months at the time, and when you got out wasn't nothing but skin and bones and scarcely able to walk.

Half the time a slave didn't know that he was sold 'til the massa'd call him to the Big House and tell him he had a new master. Every time that one was sold the rest of em'd say, "I hopes next time'll be me." They thought you'd git a chance to run away to the free states. I heerd my mammy say that when she come from Virginny that she come on a boat built outen logs. She say she never was so sick in all her life. I seed a whole wagonload of slaves come through our farm one day what was on their way to Arkansas. They was the most I ever seed travel at the same time.

The white folks didn't 'low us to even look at a book. They would scold and sometimes whup us iffen they caught us with our head in a book. One thing I sho'ly did want to do was to learn to read and write. Massa Jim promised to teach us to read and write, but he never had the time.

There warn't but one church on the place what I lived on, and the colored and the white both went to hit. You know we was never 'lowed to go to church withouten some of the white folks with us. [Alabama law prior to the Civil War forbade black religious assemblies without the presence of whites. This law was passed because slaveowners worried that the wrong kind of preaching and singing could lead to unreast or even slave revolts.] We warn't even 'lowed to talk with nobody from another farm. Iffen you did, you git one of the worst whuppings of your life. After Freedom, Massa Jim told us they was afraid we'd git together and try to run away to the North.

A few years 'fore the war my pappy learnt to read the Bible. Whenever we would go to church he would read to us and we'd sing. Bout the most popular songs they sung was "Steal Away" and "I Wonder Whar Good Ol' Daniel Was." "Steal Away" is might nigh played out, so I'll sing hit for you. Hit goes lak this:

I wonder whar was good ol' Dan'el,
I wonder whar was good ol' Dan'el,
I wonder whar was thankin' [thinking] Peter,
I wonder whar was thankin' Peter,

(Chorus)
I'm going away, goin' away,
I'm goin' away, goin' away,
I wonder whar was weepin' Mary,
I wonder whar was weepin' Mary,
I'm goin' away to live forever,
I'll never turn back no mo'.

The blacks and the whites would have the terriblest battles sometimes. The slaves would git tired of the way they was treated and try to slip off to the North. The patterollers'd ketch the colored folks and lock em up 'til the owner come after them.

I had a cousin to run away one time. Him and another fellow had got way up in Virginny 'fore Massa Jim found out whar they was. Soon as Massa Jim found the whar'bouts of George he went after him. When Massa Jim gits to George, George pretended like he didn't know Massa Jim.

Massa Jim ask him, "George, don't you know me?"

George he say, "I never seen you 'fore in my life."

Then they ask George and em whar did they come from. George and this other fellow look up in the sky and say, "I come from above, whar all is love."

Iffen they had owned they knowed Massa Jim he could have brung em back home. My pappy tried to git away the same time as George and em did, but he couldn't see how to take us chillun with him, so he had to stay with us.

Iffen a slave was cotched out after nine o'clock he was whupped. They didn't 'low nobody out after hit was dark lessen he had a pass from the massa. One night 'fore George and this fellow runned away, George tried to git over to the bunk whar he lived and one of the overseers seen him and they put him in the nigger box for three weeks. Jes as soon as he got out again, George and this Ezra slipped off. They had a sign that they would give each other every night after sundown. George would hang the lantern in the window, and then he would take hit outen the window and hang hit right back in there again. I couldn't never make no sense outen hit. I axed him one day what he was a-doing that for. He say that 'fore long I'd know zackly what it all about.

After the day's work was over, the slaves didn't have nothing to do but go to bed. In fact, they didn't feel like doing nothing else. On Sat'day they washed so's they could have some clean clothes to wear the coming week. We worked all day every day cep'n some Sat'days, we had a half-day off then. Us didn't get many and only when us ask for em. On Sundays us jes laid round most all day. Us didn't git no pleasure outen going to church, cause we warn't 'lowed to say nothing. Sometimes even on Christmas us didn't get no rest. I remembers one Christmas us had to build a lime kiln. When us git a holiday, us rested. Iffen there was a wedding or a funeral on our plantation us went. Otherways, we don't go nowhar.

The war come when I was a big gal. I remember that my uncle and cousin j'ined in with the Yankees to fight for the freedom. The Yankees come to our place and runned Massa Jim away and took the house for a hospital. They took all of Massa Jim's clothes and gived them to some of their friends. They burned up all the cotton, hay, peas, and everything that was in the barns. They made all the white folks cook for the colored and then serve em while they et. The Yankees made em do for us like we done them. They showed the white folks what hit was to work for somebody else. They stayed on our place for the longest. When they did leave, there warn't a mouthful to eat in the whole house. When the war was over, Massa Jim told us that we had to find some'eres else to live. Course some of my folks had already gone when he come home. Us left Massa Jim's and moved to another farm. We got pay for the work what we did on this other place.

Right after the war the Ku Klux got after the colored folks. They would come to our houses and scare us most to death. They would take some of the niggers out and whup em and those that they didn't whup they tied up by their fingers and toes. These Ku Klux would come to our windows at night and say, "Your time ain't long a-coming." The Ku Klux got so bad that they would even git us in the daytime. They took some of the niggers and throwed em in the river to drown. They kept this up 'til some folks from the North come down and put a stop to hit.

I married Nelson Grandberry. The wedding was private. I don't have no chilluns, but my husband got four. I haven't heered from any of em in a long time now. I guess they all daid.

Abe Lincoln was the best president this country ever had. Iffen hit hadn't been for him we'd still be slaves right now. I don't think so much of Jeff Davis cause he tried to keep us slaves. Booker T. Washington was one of the greatest niggers that ever lived, he tried to raise the standard of the race.

I j'ined at the church cause the Bible says that all people should j'in the church and be Christians. Jesus Christ set up the church and said that everybody what wanted to be saved to come unto him. Sin is the cause of the world being in the fix that hit's in today. The only way to fight sin is to git together. Iffen we can do away with sin right now, the world would be a paradise. In the church we learn the will of God and what He would have us do.

Sho I Believes in Spirits

Charles Hayes
MAYEVILLE

I was a little bitty nigger when the war broke out, and I belonged to Massa Ben Duncan who lived at Day's Landing on the Alabammy River. After the war my pappy and mammy stayed on the Duncan plantation and worked on sharecrops. There was a school on the grounds for us slave chilluns, and my grandmammy, Salina Duncan, taught the Bible, cause she was from Virginny and had been learnt to read and write by her mistress up there.

Marse Ben's house was the regulation plantation with slave quarters. Most of the things us used was made right there on the plantation, such as: beds, buckets, tools, soap, brogans, breeches, and chairs. Our mattresses was either made outen cornshucks or cotton bolls. Us cooked on an open fireplace, and every Sat'day night us would go to the Big House for supplies. Marse Ben was good to his slaves and he 'lowed em to have a little plot of ground next to the cabins whar they could raise their own little crop.

My mammy was a field hand, and my pappy was a mechanic. He useta be the handyman around the Big House, making everything from churns and buckets to wagon wheels. My pappy also used to play the fiddle for the white folks' dances in the Big House, and he played it for the colored frolics, too. He sho could make that thing sing.

Us useta have all sorts of cures for the sick people. For instance, us used the Jerusalem weed cooked with molasses into a candy to give to the chilluns to git rid of worms. Then us'd bile the root and make a kinda tea for the stomach worms. You know the kinds that little puppies and little chilluns has that eats all the food that goes into the stomach, and makes the chile or dog eat plenty but don't git no benefits from all they're eating. Horehound, that growed wild in Clarke County, was used for colds. Mullein tea was used for colds and swollen joints. Then there was the life-everlasting tea that was also good for colds, and horsemint tea that was good for the chills and fevers. Course, us niggers had a regular doctor that tended to us when we was downright sick, but these remedies I's telling you bout us used when warn't nothing much ailing us. It was always to the owner's interest to have the niggers in a good, healthy condition.

Does I believe in spirits? Sho I does. When Christ walked on the water, the apostles was skeered He was a spirit, but Jesus told em He warn't no spirit, that He was as 'live as they was. He told em that spirits couldn't be tetched, that they just melted when you tried to. So, Jesus musta meant that there was such a thing as spirits.

My first wife was named Alice Bush, and us had ten chilluns. My second one was named Caroline Turner, and us didn't have but eight. Both my ole women is dead now, white folks, and I stays here with one of my daughters. You see, my eyesight is almost gone due to one day when I was a-working in the forge, a hot piece of iron flew up and landed in my eye. 'Twarn't long before it started to hurting in my other eye. Now both is about to give out.

I Runned Most of the Way

Lizzie Hill
EUFAULA

I was most grown when Freedom come. My marster [Richard Dozier] and my mistress was good to all they niggers, and they raised me right. I had two little mistresses bout as old as me, and I played with them all the time and slept on a pallet in they room every night. They slept on the big bed. My clothes was jes as good and clean as theyrn, and I ate what they ate.

After Freedom come, mammy moved to Cuthbert and took me away from Old Mistress; but I runned away and went back to Mistress, and walked all the fourteen miles down the big road at night—I runned most of the way. Three times I done that, but Mammy come and took me back to work in the field every time. I wanted to stay with Old Mistress. They called her "Miss Everlina" and everybody liked her. Both my little mistressses got married and then Old Marster and Old Mistress moved off to Texas, and I ain't ever seed none of em no more. I's had a hard time working in the field since the war. 'Fore Freedom come, I never worked cep'n in the house—I was a "house girl" and didn't do no field work.

A Conjure What Didn't Work

Jake Green
COATOPA

Me and my mother and father belonged to Old Man Lam Whitehead jes a few miles from Coatopa, bout ten miles east of Livingston, Alabama. My mother was Molly Whitehead, my father was Dan Whitehead. I don't know nothing bout my grandmammy and grandpappy, but I had a heap of uncles.

Mr. Whitehead owned Dirtin Ferry down to Belmont, and they had a darky there named Dick what claim sick all the time. So the massa man said, "Dick, damn it, go to the house. I can't get no work out of you." So Dick went on.

He was a fiddler so they just took his victuals to him for seven years. Then one day Old Massa say to the overseer man, "Let's slip up there and see what Dick doing." So they did, and there sot Dick, fat as he could be a-playing the fiddle and a-singing,

Fool my massa seven years.
Gwiner fool him seven mo.
Hey diddle, the diddle, the diddle, the do.

Bout that time Old Massa poked his head in the door and said, "Damn iffen you will. Come on outen there, you black rascal, and go to work," and I never heard of Dick complaining no more.

But they wasn't so mean. Sometimes us got whipped but Massa had four men he didn't 'low nobody to hit, white or black. They was Uncle Arch, he was the main carriage driver; my father, he was the house servant; Uncle Julius, the foreman of the plow hands; and Uncle Edwards, the foreman of the hoe hands. Whenever anybody wanted to hire anybody to work or pick, the massa send them out and hire em by the day to chop cotton or pick. Any them four niggers could chop as much cotton in a day as the mule could plow. Whenever they'd stop the plow at twelve o'clock, them niggers was right there to lay the hoe handles on the plow, and that's chopping. All four could pick a bale of cotton a day. Whenever anybody say, "Mr. Whitehead, I want a bale of cotton picked today," he send them four men and they could pick five hundred pounds apiece and leave the sun still running. They was pickers in them days!

Course all of us got up 'fore day. Twarn't nothing strange to be standing in the field by your plow waiting for the sun to come up. Everybody was early risers in them days!

They was pretty good to us, but Ole Mr. Buck Brasefiel', what had a plantation j'ining us'n, was so mean to his'n that warn't nothing for em to run away. One nigger, Rich Parker, runned off one time and whilst he gone he seed a hoodoo man, so when he got back, Mr. Brasefiel' took sick and stayed sick two or three weeks. Some of the darkies told him, "Rich been to the hoodoo doctor." So Mr. Brasefiel' got up outen that bed and come a-yelling in the field, "You thought you had Old Buck, but by God he rose ag'in!" Them niggers was so skeered, they squatted in the field just like partridges, and some of em whispered, "I wish to God he had a-died."

'Twarn't long after that come Surrender, but that nigger done left there, and didn't nobody know whar Parker was at. Some of the niggers done bought and paid for they mule, and me and Pappy was renting and working on shares, when here come Parker, jes heared bout Surrender. He say, "Why didn't somebody come tell me 'twas Surrender?" Then he start a-singing,

Slav'ry chain, slav'ry chain
Thank God a'mighty I'm free at las',
Free at las', free at las'
Thank God a'mighty I'm free at las'.

But that warn't none of Old Massa's niggers. He had one call John, and hit come a traveler and stayed all night. Old Massa pointed out John and said, "He ain't never told me a lie in his life." The traveler bet Massa a hundred dollars against four bits [fifty cents] he'd ketch John in a lie 'fore he left. Next mawning at the table the mice was pretty bad, so the traveler caught one by the tail and put him inside a kiver-lid ["kiver" means "cover"] dish what was setting there on the table, and he told Old Massa tell John he could eat somep'n out of every dish after they got through but that kiver-lid one, and not to take the kiver offen hit.

And John said, "No suh, I won't." But John jes nachully had to see what was in that dish, so he raise the lid and out hopped the mouse. Then here come Old Massa and axed John iffen he done what he told him not to do, and John 'nied hit. Then the traveler look in the dish and the mouse warn't there, and he said, "See there, John been lying to you all the time. You jes ain't knowed it," and I reckon he right, cause us had to lie.

The Yankees Was a Harricane

Cornelia Robinson
OPELIKA

I 'members a storm we had. I call it a harricane, but it was really the Yankees comin' through. Chile, them Yankees come through and cleaned out the smokehouse, even left the lard bucket as clean as your hand. Old Marster took his best horses and mules to the big swamp, and the Yankees couldn't find them. But they tore up everything they couldn't take with em. They poured all the syrup out, and it run down the road lak water.

One poor little nigger boy was so skeered that when

he went out to get up the cows and when he couldn't find some of em, he laid down in a hollow stump and nearly froze to death. They had to thaw him out in the branch, but he was powerful sick. He wasn't no-account after that.

I remember that Old Missus saved all her jewels and such from the Yankees. She brung them out to the nigger cabins and hid them amongst us.

I 'members the high, four-poster beds we used to sometimes sleep on. I was so little that I had to crawl into them with the help of a stool. I 'members that the mud fireplaces of early times was far back, deep and wide. All the little niggers was fed milk and bread, with the bread crumbled in. Us also had pot liquor and greens.

Our clothes were muslin and calico for the hot weather; and then in winter we had linty [linsey-woolsey] cloth, part wool and part cotton, homespun. We raised the sheep, too, but we didn't wear no clothes hardly in hot weather.

Us sho' did have a good marster and mistress. They give us all the clothes and food we needed and gave us medicine. Us wore asefidity [asafetida] and pennies around our necks to help us not get sick.

They taught my mother to read and write, too. Not many done that. She'd read the Bible to us little niggers and give prayers. After slavery, we had schools. I remember that George Hawkins and his wife taught it.

If the slaves went off the plantation without a pass, the paterollers would catch em and beat em powerful bad. If the niggers would outrun the paterollers and git home first they couldn't be whupped. They had dogs called "nigger hounds," same like they had bird dogs, and they would track the slaves and bring them back home.

I 'members my mother goin' to cornshuckin's. Course they got us little niggers to bed before they went but they sho' sounded like they were having a big time, hollerin' and singin'. Us went to the white folks' church in the afternoon, and the Reverend Gardner was a mighty good preacher. When any of us niggers died, Marster was good to us and let all the niggers quit and attend the burial. They made the coffins at home and would black them with soot.

Us had an old quack herb doctor on the place. Some bad boys went up to his house one night and poured a whole lot of the medicine down him. And honey, that old man died the next day.

We Et Like Li'l Pigs

Annie Stanton
MOBILE

Honey, folks talkin' bout Depression now don't know nothin' bout hard times. In them days folks didn't have nothing cepting what they made. Even if you had a mint of money, there was nothin' to buy. We made the candles to burn by tying strings on the sticks and puttin' them down in melted tallow in molds. In them times, we had no matches. We made fire by strikin' flint rocks together, and the fire dropping on cotton. Don't know whether these rocks were ones that the Indians left or not, but they was different from other rocks. People useta to carry them and the cotton roun' in boxes somep'n lak snuff boxes to keep the cotton dry. Sometimes when they couldn't get the fire no odder way, they would put the cotton in the fireplace and shoot up in there and set hit on fire. The fust matches and lantern I ever seed was when the Yankees come to the place. I thought they was two officers, cause they had the matches and lantern. Two years later I was freed, and 'twas then I seed my first lamp.

The men did most of the farm work. They planted cotton, corn, potatoes, cane, peas, and pumpkins, and they ginned the cotton by hitching four hosses to the gin, and they run hit that way. Lord, I guess we had 'nough to eat, but 'tweren't much, cause I 'members when we was chillun we had a big wooden tray that they put the food in and us all set round that and et like li'l pigs. The rations for a week was three pounds of meat, one peck of meal, potatoes, and syrup.

At Christmastimes the overseer called all the men and women in and give each woman a dress, a head handker-chief, and to the men he gave a hat, knife, and a bottle of whiskey. The overseer also give us flour and sugar for Christmas, and I 'members one Christmas when I was a li'l gal after the overseer give all the women a dress there was a short piece of cloth left and he give that to me.

The slaves went to the white folks' church, and sot on the seats on the outside. That church was a hewed-log building. After the white folks through preaching, then the colored preacher would preach. Sometimes the colored would have church when the white folks didn't, and then the slave would have to get a pass from his owner, cause there would be some mean folks that would beat the niggers if they didn't have a pass from their owners or bosses.

I's never heered of no hoodoo stuff 'til in late years. They's mo' of that foolishness now. The hoodoos doctors, what is allus goin' round foolin' folks out of they money, looks lak the dogs might of had them they is so turrible lookin'. I don't believes in them. Us folks a long time ago never have no money fo' them to git. Us had to make our own medicine. When the babies had the colic us would tie soot up in a rag and boil it, and then give them the water, and to ease the prickly heat us used rotten wood powdered up fine.

Cornshuckin'
Was the Greates' Thing

George Strickland
OPELIKA

I was nine years old when us niggers was set free. Before that time us refugeed from Mississippi to Mobile, then to Selma, then to Montgomery, and from there to Uchie, near Columbus, Georgia, whar we stayed 'til us was freed. My mammy and daddy come from Mississippi. They was Cleveland and Eve Strickland, and thar was four of us chilluns—Will, Sam, Missouri, and me.

Us quarters had dirt floors and was in two long rows with a street between. On the east side of the settlement was the barns, shops, and such-like. The beds was boxed up and nailed to the wall, then they was filled with pine straw.

They fed us li'l niggers in wood troughs made of pop-lar. The cook in the Big House cooked pots of greens and poured pot liquor and all in the troughs. Us et hit with mussel shells or with us's hands or gourds. Our womenfolks would boil the gourds to keep them from being bitter. Us's had a two-acre pasture that us would turn under in the fall and plant hit in turnips. They growed nearly as big as a gallon bucket. The well didn't have no windlass but had a lever with a bucket fastened on one end, and we would hold to the other end to dip the bucket in the water.

On Sunday mornin' they gives us biscuits for breakfast, which was so rare that we would try to beat the others outen they'n. They gived us clothes every Sat'day night, and the winter clothes had some cow hair in em to make em warm.

Miss Polly lived up in a big house. The logs was hewed and split and lined on each side. The logs stood on their sides and didn't lay flat. They chilluns was Mary, Laura, Sallie, Wiley, George, and Lougene.

You sho' had to stay at home and work. They had bout a hundred slaves and would wake them up by beating on a big piece of sheet iron with a long piece of steel. When Old Marse went off to preach, the overseer was mean and whupped the niggers so bad Mistress runned him off. When they whupped the niggers they would tie them to a tree and whup them good. When slaves would be very bad they would chain them out all night.

When they was sold they would put em on a stand or block, as they called hit, and they would roll up they sleeves to see the muscles. Then they bid on them and bought them for bout $1,000 to $1,500 apiece.

The womenfolks had a big time quiltin's with somebody a'playin' on ol' gourds with horsehair strings, called old-gourd-and-horsehair dance.

Cornshuckin' was the greates' thing of all. Old Marse took a jug of liquor round and got them tight and when they got full they would heist him up and down, tote him round and holler. Then the fun started, and they would play the old-gourd-and-horsehair dance, the handsaw, and case knife. They could run they hand up and down the saw to change the tune. The others would follow. Us chilluns was asleep then, but us had our good times hidin' the switch and playin' hand-over ball. They sho' skeer us nearly into fits with tales of Rawhead and Bloody-Bones.

Us traveled in ox carts, and I first rid on a stage when I went to Uchie. Oncet they piled everythin' on wagons and put all us li'l niggers on top. Us rations was kivvered over with sheets. Then they tuk us off and us stayed three days and nights. Old Marsa took one of the fellers with him to be on the front line to help keep off the Injuns, so us chilluns b'lieved.

Our church was nearby and us sot next to the door. Mistress called up all the li'l niggers, talked to them and had prayer. The others had prayer meeting oncet a week. I's never took a oath ner teched nothin' didn't belong to me in all my life. I's allus tried to live under the correction of the Lord. Hit was the plans of God to free us niggers, and not Abraham Lincoln's.

This Was That Long Ago

William Henry "Bill" Towns
TUSCUMBIA

It's been so long, I don't 'member much. I was born in Tuscumbia, Alabama, December 7, 1854. My mother was Jane Smoots. She come from Baltimore, Maryland. My father was Joe Towns, and he come from Huntsville, Alabama.

I had a passel of brothers and sisters: Charlie and Bob, Betty, Kate, Lula and Nelie. There wasn't but two of us endurin' slavery. That was me and Nelie. The rest was born after slavery. Me and Nelie was Townses; the rest—Charlie, Kate, Lula, Bob, and Betty—was Joneses. How that come bout was this a-way: Durin' slavery my father was sold to another slave owner. After the war my mother married Frank Jones; then these other chillun was born.

The Big House was a two-story house; white like most houses durin' that time. On the north side set a great, big barn, where all the stock and stuff that was raised was kept. Off to the southwest of the barn and west of the Big House set bout five or six log houses. These house was built facing a space of ground in the center of a square. Anybody could stand in his front door and see in at the front of the other houses.

Sometimes durin' the week and on Sunday, too, the people would git together out in this square and talk 'fore goin' to bed. The chillun what was too young to work was always out in the front playin'. Jes acrost from our place was another with the quarters built most the same as ourn cepting that they had a picket fence round the quarters to prevent em from runnin' away. Course Mr. Young didn't have to worry bout his hands runnin' away, cause he wasn't a mean man like some of the slaveholders was. He never spoke harsh or whupped em, and he didn't 'low nobody else to do it, neither.

I 'member one day a fellow come from another farm and spoke somep'n bout Mr. Young bein' too easy with his servants. He said, "Them damn niggers will think they is good as you iffen you keep up the rate you goin' now, Young." Mr. Young up and told him if he ever spoke like that again he'd call his bluff. Mr. Young told him that he didn't work his people like they was oxes.

All of Mr. Young's hands liked him cause he didn't make

em sleep on cornshuck mattresses, and he didn't have they meals cooked in a wash pot. A lot of the other slaves didn't know what it was to eat meat, lessen it was a holiday. Mr. Young 'lowed his people to eat just what he eat. I hear my mother tell a tale bout a man what took a meat skin and whipped his chillun's mouth with it to fool folks like they had some meat for dinner. Old Caleb told one a li'l bit bigger'n that, though. He said one night him and a feller was comin' from prayer meeting, and they runned 'crost a possum settin' in the root of a tree by the side of the road. He say he stopped to git him, and the other feller told him he wouldn't bother with him cause he wouldn't git none of him nohow. Caleb axed him why he said that. He said, "Cause your old master is gwine take him jes soon as you git home with him." Caleb told him that Mr. Young wasn't that kinder man. The other feller helped Caleb to ketch that possum, and he got a piece of him the next night when ever'body come in from the field. Caleb said the old feller enjoyed the meat so much that he wished he took him and his family the whole possum.

We didn't live so far from Big Spring Creek. Course, we didn't do no fishin', cause we younguns had to 'tend gaps [a makeshift gate through a fence] to keep the cattle offen the crops. The grownups had to go to the field. Life was kinder happy durin' slavery cause we never knowed nothing bout any other life or freedom. All we knowed was work from one end of the year to the other, ceptin' on holidays. Then we'd have to go to church or set around the fire and listen to the old folks tell stories. The grownups would go to a dance or do somep'n else for indertainment. Course, us younguns got a heap of pleasure outen them fairy tales that was told us by the older ones. I know Ma and them useta tell some of the awf'lest tales. I'd be 'fraid to go from one part of the house to the other withouten somebody with me. Us younguns would had to play some sort of game for indertainment. There was a whole lot of games and riddles to be played them days. It have been so long sence I played any of em I's disremembers the biggest part of em. I 'members a song or two and a few riddles what old Caleb use to tell us. The song goes somep'n like this:

> Saturday night and Sunday, too
> Had a yaller gal on my mind.
> Monday comin', break of day
> White folks had me gwine.

The riddles was like this:

> Slick as a mole, black as coal,
> Got a great long tail like a thunder hole.
> (skillet)

> Crooked as a rainbow, teeth lak a cat,
> Guess all of your life but you can't guess that.
> (blackberrry bush)

> Grows in the winter, dies in the spring,

Lives with the root stickin' straight up.
(icicle)

There was another song what Caleb useta sing. It goes like this:

Whar you gwine, buzzard? Whar you gwine, crow?
Gwine down to the river to the jes so.

There was a whole lot more to that song what I dis-remembers.

Another song what comes to my min' is:

Hawk and the buzzard went down to the law;
When the hawk got back he had a broken jaw.
Lady's pocketbook on the judge's bench
Haden' had no use for a pocketbook since.

Sometimes I visits with Ol' Mingo White, and me and him talks over them days that me and him was boys. We gits to talkin' and 'fore you knows it Old Mingo is crying lak a baby. 'Cording to what he says he is lucky ter be a-livin'. This is one thing I never likes to talk bout. When slavery was goin' on it was all right for me cause I never had it hard, but it jes wan't right to treat human bein's that way. If we hadn't a-had to work and slave for nothin' we might have somep'n to show for what we did do, and wouldn't have to live from pillar to post [aimlessly from place to place] now.

Speakin' of clothin', everything that we wore back then was made by han'. Many a night my ma useta set and spin with a spindle. I have set and done the cardin' for her so she could git her task done. In the summer we would wear underwear what was made outen cotton. In the winter it was made outen flannel. The shoes was made of cowhide what was tanned right there on the place. Them was the hardest shoes I ever seen. Sometimes they'd wear out 'fore they was any ways soft, and then sometimes after they was wore out you couldn't hardly bend em. Some of the hands would go barefooted until the fall and then wear shoes. Slippers wasn't wore then. The fust pair of slippers I 'members havin' was the ones what I bought for my weddin'. They didn't cost but a dollar and six bits. My weddin' suit didn't cost but eight dollars, and a straw hat to match it cost six bits.

As I said afore, Massa Young and Old Mistress was mighty good folks on 'count of they never whupped any of they hands. Iffen there was one that would give trouble they would git rid of him. The overseer had to be kind to the hands or else he was outen a job. The chillun was mighty nice, too. Ever' time they went to town or to the sto' they would bring us younguns some candy or somep'n. Joinin' our farm was a farm whar the slaves fared lak dogs. They was always beating on some of them.

Everybody worked hard durin' that time. That was all we thought we was spose to do, but Abe Lincoln taught us better'n that. Some say that Abe wasn't interested so much in freein' the slaves as he was in savin' the Union. Don't make no difference, he sho' done a big thing. Some of the slaveholders would double the proportion of work so as to git to whip em when night come. I heard my maw say after slavery that they jes whupped the slaves so much to keep em cowed down and cause they might have fought for Freedom much sooner'n it did come.

Caleb come from New Orleans. He say that many a day shiploads of slaves was unloaded there and sold to the one offerin' the mos' money for them. They had big chains and shackles on them to keep em from gittin' away. Sometime they would have to go a long ways to git to the farm. They would go in a wagon or on hossback.

Talk bout learnin' to read and write, why, iffen we so much as spoke of learnin' to read and write we was scolded lak the devil. Iffen we was caught lookin' in a book we was treated same as iffen we had killed somebody. A servant better not be caught lookin' in a book; didn't make no difference if you wasn't doin' nothin' but lookin' at the pictures.

We went to the same church as the white folks; only in the evenin' after the white folks. The white folks would go along and read the Bible for the preacher, and to keep em from talking of things that might help them to git free. They would sing songs like "Steal Away," "Been Toilin' at the Hill So Long," and "Old-Time Religion."

Ever' once in a while slaves would run away to the North. Most times they was caught and brought back. Sometimes they would git desperate and would kill themselves 'fore they would stand to be brought back. One time I heard of a slave that had escaped and when they tried to ketch him he jumped in the creek and drown hisself. He was brought from over in Georgia. He hadn't been in Alabama long 'fore him and two more tried to 'scape; two of em was caught and brought back but the other one went to the land of sweet dreams.

After the day's work was done and all had eat, the slaves had to go to bed. Most slaves worked on Sat'day jes lak they did on Monday; that was from can to can't, or from sun to sun. Mr. Young never worked his slaves 'til dark on Sat'day. He always let em quit round four o'clock. We would spen' this time washin' and bathin' to git ready for church on Sunday. The hands celebrated every holiday that their white folks celebrated. There wasn't much to do for entertainment, ceptin' what I's already said. Ever' Christmas we'd go to the Big House and git our present, cause Old Mistress always give us one.

Slaves never got sick much, but when they did they got the best. There was always a nurse on the farm, and when a slave got sick they was right there to give em treatments. Back in those days they used all sorts of roots and yarbs for medicine. Peach-tree leaves was one of the most often. Sassafras was another what was used often; hit was used mostly in the spring, made in tea. Azzafitty [asafetida] was another that was use to keep you from havin' asthma. Hit was wore round the neck in a li'l bag. Prickler ash [prickly ash] was another what was tooken in the spring. Hit was 'spose to clean the blood. Some of the folks would use brass, copper, and dimes with holes in em to keep from havin' their rheumatiz.

I was seven years old when the war commence. I 'members Mrs. Young said when the Yankees come they was goin' to ast us iffen they had been good to us. She said that they was goin' to ast us all bout how much money they had and how many slaves what they owned. She told us to say they was po' folks and that they didn't have no money. I 'member my mother said that she holped Mr. Young and them to hide their money some'eres in a well that wasn't being used cause it gone dry. Them Yankees sho' did clean up whar they went along. They would ketch chickens by the bunches and kill em and then turn round and make the old mistress clean em and cook for em. Them Yankees set fire to bales and bales of cotton. They took the white folks' clothes and did away with em. Sometimes they would tear em up or give them to the slaves to wear.

Jes after the war we was turned loose to go for ourself. What I mean by that, we was free. I didn't mean that we lef' Mr. Young's cause we stayed with him for the longest after slavery was over.

My fust work was in a blacksmith shop down on West Sixth Street. I worked for fifty cents a day until I learned the trade. After I worked at the blacksmith shop for about two years I took up carpenter work. I served apprentice for three years. I followed carpent'ing the rest of my life.

I married Lizzie Anderson when I was twenty-one years old. She wasn't but seventeen. We didn't have no big wedding, jes had the family there. I raised ten chillun up until April the twenty-fourth. That's when William Henry died. My chilluns doin' pretty well in life. There's two of my sons what's doctors; one is a carpenter. The other one is Grand Orator of the Shriners. My gals is doin' fine, too. Three of em is been schoolteachers, one a beauty cult'ist, and the other is a nurse. I feels satisfied bout my chillun now. They seems to be able to make a livin' for theyselves pretty well.

I thinks Abe Lincoln was a mighty fine man even if he was tryin' to save the Union. I don't like to talk bout this that have done happened. It done passed so I don't say much bout it, 'specially the presidents, cause it might cause a 'sturbance right now. All men means well, but some of em ain't broadminded nough to do anythin' for nobody but themselfs. Any man that tries to help humanity is a good man.

Hongry for Punkin Pie

Adeline Hodges
MOBILE

The first white people I belonged to was a man named Jones, who was a colonel in the war. I was jes big enough to tote water to the field to the folks working and to mind the gaps in the fence to keep the cattle out when they was gathering the crops. I don't expect you knows anything bout those kind of fences. They was built of rails, and when they was gathering the crops they jes took down one section of the fence so the wagons could git through.

After the war broke out, Old Marster Jones went off to hit, and I 'members the day he left. He come to the field to tell all the hands goodbye, with a big white plume on his hat. That was in Bolivar County, Mississippi. After Old

Marster Jones left for the war, then the nigger drivers and overseer begun to drive us round lak droves of cattle. Every time they would hear the Yankees was coming they would take us out in the woods and hide us. Finally they sold us after carrying us away from Bolivar County. Some of us was sold to people in Demopolis, Alabama, and Atlanta, Georgia, and some to folks in Meridian and Shubuta, Mississippi. I don't anymore know whar my own folks went to than you does.

I 'members afore leaving Old Mister Jones's place how they grabbed up all the chillun that was too little to walk and put us in wagons. Then the older folks had to walk, and they marched all day long. Then at night they would strike camp. I has seen the young niggers what was liable to run away with their legs chained to a tree or the wagon wheels. They would rake up straw and throw a quilt over hit and lie that way all night, while us chillun slep' in the wagons.

When us come to the big river at Demopolis, Alabama, I 'members seeing the big steamboats there, and they said the soldiers was going away on them. Hit was in Demopolis us was sold, and a man named Ned Collins of Shubuta, Mississippi, bought me.

I jes hates to have to weigh anything today, cause I 'members so well that each day that the slaves was given a certain number of pounds of cotton to pick. When weighing-up time come and you didn't have the number of pounds set aside, you may be sho that you was going to be whupped.

But hit wasn't all bad times cause us did have plenty to

eat, 'specially at hog-killing time. They would have days of hog killing, and the slaves would bake their bread and come with pots, pepper, and salt. After cleaning the hogs, they would give us the livers and lights (livers and lungs), and us would cook them over a fire out in the open, and hit sho was good eating. The usual 'lowance a week of pickled pork was six or seven pounds, and iffen you had a big family of chillun they give you more. Then they give you a peck of meal, sweet taters, sorghum syrup, and plenty of buttermilk. At Christmastimes, they give you extra syrup to make cakes with and sweet taters to make tater pone. And Lord, they would have big cribs of punkins. Hit makes me hongry to think bout them good old punkin pies.

And did they raise chickens? You knows in Mississippi that the minks was bad about killing them. I 'members one time the minks got in the chicken house and killed nearly every chicken on the place. Old Mister Jones had the cook to clean and cook them, and he come out the field and eat with them to let the slaves know that hit was all right. Then we had them good old cushaws [varieties of squash] and lye hominy [whole or ground hulled corn from which the bran and germ have been removed by bleaching the whole kernels in a lye bath], too.

The clothes was made out of homespun in one piece. I 'members I allus had mine split up the side so I could git bout in a hurry. The women had pantalettes made and tied to their knees to wear in the fields to keep dew off their legs. The shoes was made of cowhide and was called red russets. The way they got them darker was to take a hog gristle and hang it up in the chimley. When hit git full of soot, we rub the shoes with that. Then they used the darker shoes for their Sunday best.

Lord, yes, they hunted in them times. Up in them swamps in Mississippi there was bears as big as cows, and deers aplenty. They both was bad about coming in the cornfields and tearing down the corn. You could hear them at nights out in the fields. They also caught plenty of possums and coons.

Of course us got sick, but they had the doctor. In those days the doctor would cup you and bleed you. I seen many a person cupped. The doctor had a little square-looking block of wood with tiny little knifes attached to hit. On top was a trigger lak is on a gun, and the doctor would put the block of wood at the nape of their neck and pull that trigger. Then he have a piece of cotton with somep'n on it to stop the blood when he had cupped you long enough. They would allus give us calumus [calomel] to clean us out, and then the next mawning they give us a big bowl of gruel made out of meal and milk. Then us'd be all right.

The slaves warn't 'lowed to go to church, but they would whisper round and all meet in the woods and pray. The only time I 'members my paw was one time when I was a li'l chile, he set me on a log by him and prayed, and I knows that was where the seeds of religion was planted in my mind. Today I's happy to tell folks bout Jesus and thank Him for his goodness to me. Hit won't be long 'til I meet Him face to face and thank Him.

I Had Many Masters

Caroline Holland
MONTGOMERY

I was borned in 1849 on Mr. Will Wright's plantation on the Mount Meigs road. Massa Will had a big slave house and us niggers sho use to have a good time playing round down at the slave quarters. We had a row of houses two stories high, and they was filled with all sorts of niggers. When I was twelve years old, I was made nuss for my mistress's little girl and at the first I couldn't do nothing but rock the cradle. I didn't know how to hold the baby. Us niggers had guardians that look after us like they did after the hosses and cows and pigs. [Under Alabama law, minors could not own property. An adult had to be the legal guardian of a slave owned by a child until the child reached the age of majority]

One night after we had all gone to bed I heered a noise at the window and when I look up there was a man climbing in. Even though I could scarce see him I knowed he was a nigger. I could hear my mistress a-breathing, and the baby was sound sleep, too. I started to yell out but I thought that the nigger would kill us all so I jes kept quiet. He come in the window and he see us a-sleeping there, and all of a sudden I knowed who it was. "Jade," I whispers, "What you a-doing here?" He come to my bed and put his rough hand over my mouth.

"Listen you black pickaninny, you tell that you saw me here and I'll kill you," he say. "I throw yo' hide to the snakes in the swamp. Now shet up."

With that he went to the dresser and taken Mistress's moneybag. After that he went to the window and climb down the ladder, and I didn't do nothing but shake myself nearly to death from fright. The next day the overseer and the patterollers went a-searching through the slave quarters, and they found the moneybag under Jade's cot. They took him and whupped him for near fifteen minutes. We could hear him holler way up at the Big House. Jade, he never got over that whupping. He died three days later. He was a good nigger, 'pear to me like, and the best blacksmith in the whole county. I kept a-wondering what made him want to steal that purse. Then I found out later he was going to pay a white man to carry him over the line to the northern states. Jade just had too big ideas for a nigger. I useta see Jade's ghost a-walking out in the garden in the moonlight; sometime he sit on the fence and look at his old cabin, then sometime he stroll off down the cottonfield. When the Lawd git through punishing him for stealing that money, I guess he won't make us no mo' visits. He just go right on in heaven. That's what ghosts is, you know: peoples that can't quite git in heaven, and they have to stroll round little longer on the outside repenting.

Soon after that my guardian took me to Tallahassee when the massa died. My guardian was a good man. He was always making speeches for the slaves to stay under bondage 'til they was twenty-one. One day he was in front of a store talking bout the slaves, and a man come up to him and said he don't like the way Captain Clanton talk (that was my guardian's name). Captain Clanton ask him what he going to do bout it, and the man took out a pistol and kilt the captain right there on the spot.

Then I was sold to another man, a Mr. Williamson, bout the time the war broke loose, and Massa Williamson took me over to live with some mo' peoples. He said he had more slaves than he could take care of. This was the Abernathy plantation. While the massa was a-standing in the slave quarters a-talking to Mr. Abernathy, I noticed a boy with a bad eye. I didn't like him at all, and I told the massa I don't want to stay, cause I didn't like the way that boy Lum with the bad eye looked at me. Then Mr. Abernathy brung up a boy bout seventeen year old; a big strong-looking boy named Jeff. He say, "Jeff, look out after Carrie here. Don't let her git into no trouble." From that time 'til bout five year ago, Jeff he always look after me, cause after the war I married him. Now I ain't got nobody but myself.

The Patriarch Abraham
Saw the Stars Fall

Abraham Jones
VILLAGE SPRINGS

Yes, sir, I saw the stars fall. [This meteor shower on November 13, 1833, is memorialized in lore, song, and Alabama license plates as the night "stars fell on Alabama." Jones claimed to have been born August 1, 1825, in Russell County, Alabama, making him 112 when interviewed in 1937.] Some folks say they didn't never fall but I seen em. They fell jes like pitch from a torch, z-z-z-z-zip, z-z-z-z-zip, and big cracks come in the ground. I was settin' on the end of the porch, and I watched em. There was so many grown people crowdin' into the house, warn't no use fer me to try to git in so I jes set still. We had a big sill [a wood-framing member] under our houses, more than a foot thick, and so many people crowded in the house 'til their weight broke the sill. They was cryin' and hollerin' but the stars didn't hurt nobody; they jes fell and went out, and I don't know where they went then; maybe into them cracks in the ground. The cracks stayed a long time, and it was dangerous for the people to go about at night; they might fall in the cracks. One of them I remember was two feet across and so deep they couldn't find no bottom with a long pole. I reckon them stars kept fallin' for about an hour. Folks thought the end of time was comin', and everybody got right after that.

Back at that time the country was not settled much and there was lots of Indians. My grandpappy was a full-blooded Indian, but I don't know what kind. The Indians was good people, but if they thought you had done em wrong they'd kill you right now. I saw some of them when they left that country. They women carried the babies in some sort of sacks, hung down in front of em, and the men carried some of the bigger chillun on they shoulders. They didn't have no property—just lived wild in the woods.

A few years after the stars fell, a passel of people from the other side of Columbus, Georgia, moved over and started the town of Auburn, so they could have a place for a school.

Before the war my people took me up to Blount County, and when the war come they left me to run the gristmill. I was the fust man in Alabama to try to grind a bushel of oats. I ground em, too. A lady brung the oats and ast me could I grind em, and I told her I would try. She say they didn't had nothin' for the chillun to eat. I ground the oats, and told her, "Old Mistress, I knows jes how 'tis, and I'll be glad to give you a peck of meal if you will use it." She say, "Of course I will; jes put it in with the oat meal, and I sure will appreciate it." Her husband was off to war, and she didn't had no way to feed her chillun.

I was workin' on the road a long time after the war and was tellin' the man about that when her son hear me. She had told him about it, and so he went home and told her he had found me. She sent word back for me to go to her house and let her see if I was the same man. So I went, and when she seen me she say, "Yes, he is the same man," and she called her husband and the other chillun and told em about it. Her husband say, "Well, they is jest one thing we kin do. If he ever need a place to stay or vittles to eat, we must see that he gits them."

In slavery times I belong to Massa Frank Jones, and Timothy Jones was the overseer on the place. Frank Jones had two plantations—the one where I was born and another one close to Columbus. People ast me sometimes what kind of house I was born in and I tell em I warn't born in no house; and I warn't, I was born in the middle of the big road.

It's gittin' to where it's mighty hard for me to go now and do the work to make somep'n for us to eat. I can't git about so fast and my head bother me a lot. You does git tired after a hundred years of workin'!

How to Make Em
"Teethe Easy"

Emma Jones
OPELIKA

White folks, I belonged to Marse Wiley Jones and his wife, Mistress Melba.

I lived in a little two-room log cabin with high tester beds and mattresses filled with cornshucks. Our food then was a-way better than the stuff we eats today. It was cooked on a fireplace made outen rocks with big hooks fastened into the side to swing pots round on. Us cooked hoecakes on a three-legged skillet that sot over hot coals and us had a big oven for to bake meat and cornbread in. There ain't nothin' lak it nowdays, no'm.

Old Massa had a big garden, and we useta git the vegetables we et from his garden. The folks was plenty good to us. Sometimes the mens would hunt possums, and rabbits, and wild turkeys. We sho' loved them possums smothered in taters.

Let me tell you a sho' nuff cure for a baby that's havin' a hard time teethin'. Jes put a string of coppers round he neck and he won't have no trouble at all. Us useta do that to the little white chilluns and the black uns, too; 'specially in hot weather when they jes seem to have the misery.

After us got to be big gals, us wore cotton dresses and drawers in hot weather, and when it git cold we had to wear long drawers, and homespun wool dresses, and home-knitted socks, and shoes that the cobbler made in his shop. You know, white folks, we useta make near bout everything that was needed to run a body right on our plantation. Us had everything. On Sunday us wore gingham and calico dresses, and I married in a Swiss dress.

I worked as a house gal, and when Miss Sarah married I went with her to nuss her chilluns. Besides Miss Sarah there was Mista Billy, Mista Crick, Miss Lucy, and Miss Emma. They had two uncles and a aunt of theirs lived there, too.

We had a happy family. At night some of the house niggers would gather round the fire, and Mistress would read us the scriptures, and the white chilluns git tired and slip out the door, but us little niggers couldn't 'ford to do that; us had to stay there whether us liked it or not. Sometimes the massa let the niggers dance and frolic on Saturday nights, but we warn't 'lowed to go offen the plantation, none 'ceptin' the ones that had a wife or hus-band on another plantation; then they could only stay for a short time. Sometimes us could go off to church, and I remembers a baptizin' in the creek. Some of them niggers most got themselves drowned. They warn't used to so much water, and they would come up outen the creek a-spittin' and a-coughin' lak the devil had a-holt of em. There was so much shoutin' I 'spose everybody for ten miles round could hear them niggers a-carrying on in the creek.

During the war, my mammy helped spin cotton for the soldiers' clothes, and when the Yankees come through, us hid all the valuables in the woods. Us had to feed them and their hosses, too. They et up near bout everything we had on the place.

There warn't no schools in them days for us colored folks. Us learned from the scriptures, and by listening to the white folks talk.

Cures and "Cunjer"

Dellie Lewis
WASHINGTON COUNTY

To begin at the beginnin', white folks, I was bawn on the plantation of Winston Hunter at Sunflower in Washington County, Alabama. It's on the Southern Railroad. The fust thing I remembers was when the Grand Trunk Railroad cut their right-of-way through near Sunflower. They had a chain gang of prisoners that warn't slaves a-working on the road, and me and another little nigger gal was sont with big cans of buttermilk to sell em. One day a handsome white gentleman rode to our house and axed me for a drink of cool water. He was the foreman on the road. Jes as soon as I handed it to him he done fell offen his hoss on the ground.

I run to the mistress and she got some of the niggers round the place to carry the gentleman to the Big House, and do you know it, white folks, that man, he never open his eyes again! He kept a-calling the mistress his mammy, but he never open his eyes to see that she warn't his mammy. He died a little later with a congested chill.

Then I remembers one of the Alabama River floods that swept over the lan' and washed away lots of the food. The gov'ment sont some supplies of meat, meal, and 'lasses. The barrels was marked U.S. and one nigger, bein' tired of waitin' and bein' powerful hungry told us that the U.S. on the barrel meant US, so us commence to et. When the overseer come to give us the meat and 'lasses, us be done et it all up.

Us slaves useta git up at dawn. The overseer blowed a cow horn to call us to work. The Hunter slaves was 'lowed to go a-visiting other slaves after work hours and on Sundays, and iffen we was to meet a patteroller, and he ax us whar we from and who we belong to all us had to say was we's Hunter niggers; and that patteroller didn't do nothin', and the Hunter niggers warn't never whupped by no patteroller. Some niggers when they was kotched even though they warn't Hunter niggers, they'd say it jes the same, cause them patterollers was always 'fraid to fool long with a Hunter nigger. Massa Hunter, he was somep'n.

Durin' the Christmas celebration, us all had gifts. Us had quiltin' bees with the white folks, and iffen a white gent throwed a quilt over a white lady he was 'titled to a kiss and a hug from her. After the celebratin' we all had a big supper.

And speakin' of cures, white folks, us niggers had em. My grandmammy was a midwife, and she useta give women cloves and whiskey to ease the pain. She also give em dried watermelon seeds to get rid of the gravel in the kidneys. For night sweats Grandmammy would put an ax under the bed of the sick person with the blade a-sitting straight up. And iffen you is sick and wants to keep the visitors away, jes put a fresh-laid egg in front of the door and they won't come in. If you is anxious for yo' sweetheart to come back from a trip, put a pin in the ground with the point up and then put a egg on the point. When the insides runs outen the egg yo' sweetheart will return.

Yassuh, white folks, us useta have games. Us useta play "puss in the corner," "next do' neighbor," and "fox and geese." I kin give you some of the songs we useta sing:

Old sweet beans and barley grows,
Old sweet beans and barley grows,
You nor I nor nobody knows,
Where old sweet beans and barley grows.
Go choose yo' east,
Go choose yo' west'
Go choose the one that you love best,
If she's not here to take her part,
Choose the nex' one to yo' heart.

I is always been a 'piscopalian in belief, white folks. I married Bill Lewis when I was fifteen in Montgomery, and us had three chilluns. I is strong in my faith.

In mercy, not in wrath,
Rebuke me, gracious Lawd.
Les' when thy whole displeasure rise,
I sink beneath thy rod.

Yassuh, I remembers the war. I seed the Yankees a-marchin' through our place and down the road that led to Portland in Dallas County. They was mighty fine looking with all their brass buttons and nice-lookin' uniforms. They didn't give us much trouble. They had a cap'n that was good and kind. I heered him say that there warn't a-goin' to be no stealin' and a-tramping through folks' houses. They slept outen the yard for one night. Then they went on into Portland.

Mr. Munger was our overseer, but he had money of his own. He was better than most overseers, and there warn't no po' white trash. Them onery buckers lived further back in the woods.

When us was sick, Dr. Lewis Williams, who was the doctor of the massa, 'tended to us slaves. I remembers sitting in the doctor's lap while he tried to soothe my ailments.

Us house servants was taught to read by the white folks, but my grandmammy, Alvain Hunter, that didn't have no learnin' but that knowed the Bible back'ards and forwards, made us study. When me and my brother was learnin' outen the Blue Back Speller she say: "How's that? Go over it."

Then we would laugh and answer, "How you know? You can't read."

"Just don't sound right. The Lawd tells me when it's

right. You-all can't fool me, so don't try."

When the marriages was performed, the massa read the ceremony, and the couples would step over a broomstick for luck. Then we all had a big supper, and there was music and dancin' by the plenty.

Chasing Guinea Jim, the Runaway Slave

Josh Horn
LIVINGSTON

Us belong to Marse Ike Horn, Marse Johnnie's pa, right here on this place whar us is now, but this here didn't belong to me then, this was all Marse Ike's place. Marse Ike's gin got outer fix and we couldn't git it fixed. Colonel Lee had two gins and one of em was jes below old Turner house. Recolleck a big old hickory tree? Well, there's whar it was.

I was plenty big 'nough to drive the mules to the gin. Set on the lever and drive em, jes lak a 'lasses mill, so that night Marse Ike told us he want everybody go with him to Colonel Lee's gin next morning, and didn't want nobody to git out and go ahead of him. That held up the ginning; made us not to go to the ginhouse 'til sunup, us all standing at the gate and we heared a little fine horn up the road. Us didn't know what it meant coming to the house.

And by and by Mr. Beesley, what live not fur from Marse Ike, he rode up and had five nigger dogs, what they call em. Soon as he come, Marse Ike's hoss was saddled up and Marse Ike and him rode off down the road and the dogs with em, head of us. Us followed 'long behind em, stay close as they 'low us, to see what they was up to. When they got close to the ginhouse, right side the road, they stop us and Mr. Beesley told Old Brown to go ahead. Old Brown was the lead dog and had a bell on him. The dogs was fasten together with a rod, jes lak steers. He turn 'im loose, and then he popped the whip and hollered at Old Brown and told him "nigger." Old Brown hollered lak he hit. He want to go. And they was a fence on both sides made it a lane, so he put Old Brown over the fence on the ginhouse side and told Brown to "go ahead." He went ahead and run all around the ginhouse, and they let him in the gin-room, and he grabbled [scrambled] in the cottonseed in a hole.

Then somebody holler "Guinea Jim." I looks and I didn't see him. Didn't nobody see him, but they know that's whar he been hiding. Mr. Beesley told Old Brown he jes fooling him, and Old Brown holler agin, lak he killing him, and Mr. Beesley say: "Go git that nigger," and Old Brown started away from there lak he hadn't been hunting nothing, but he went round and round that gin, and Mr. Beesley told him hadta do better than that or he'd kill him, cause he hadn't come there for nothing.

Brown made a circle around that gin way down to the fence that time, and he was so fat he couldn't git through the fence. You know what sort of fence, a rail fence it was. Then he stop and bark for help. Now I seed this with my own eyes. They put Brown on top the fence, and he jump way out in the road, didn't stay on the fence. He jump and run up and down in the road, and couldn't find no scent of Jim.

Well, Brown come back, and this is the truth, so help me Lawd. He bark, look lak, for them to lift him up on the fence, and bless God, if that dog didn't walk that rail fence lak he walking a log, as fur as from here to that gate yonder, and track Jim jes lak he was on the ground. He fell off once, and they had to put him back, and he run his track right on to whar Jim jumped off the fence way out in the road. Old Brown run right cross the road to the other fence and treed ag'in on t'other side the road toward Konkabia. Brown walk the fence on that side the road a good piece, jes lak he done on the other side, and them other dogs, he hadn't never turned them loose.

When Brown he jump off that fence, he jump jes as fur as he can on the field side, lak he gwine ketch Jim lak a gnat or somep'n, and he never stop barking no more, jes lak he jumping a rabbit. Then, Mr. Beesley turned them other dogs loose, cause he say Old Brown done got the thing straight. And he had it straight. Them dogs run that track right on down to Konkabia and crossed it to the Blacksher side. They was a big old straw field there then and they cross it and come on through that field, all them dogs barking jes lak they looking at Jim. Directly, they come up on Jim running with a pine bresh tied behind him to drag his scent away, but it didn't bother Old Brown.

When them dogs 'gin to push him, Jim drap the bresh and runned back toward Konkabia. Now on Konkabia [Creek] there used to be beavers worse than on Sucarnatchee [Creek] now. They was a big beaver dam twixt the bridge and the Hale place, and Jim run to that beaver dam. You know when beavers build they dam, they cut down trees and let em fall in the creek, and pull in trash and bresh same as folks, to dam the water up dar 'til it's knee deep. The dogs seen him, Old Brown looking at him, jes 'fore he jump in 'bove the dam right 'mongst the trash and things they'd drug in there. Brown seed him and he jump in right behind him. Jim jes dive down under the raff, and he let he nose stick outer the water. Every once in a while Jim he put he head down under, he holding to a pole down there, and once Mr. Beesley see him, he jes let him stay there.

Brown would swim bout 'mongst the bresh, back'ards and for'ards, and terreckly Mr. Beesley told Brown, "Go git him." Then all the men got poles and dug bout in the raff hunting him. They knowed he was there, and Marse Ike had a pole gigging around trying to find him, too. Then he told Mr. Beesley to give him the hatchet and let him fix the pole. He sharpen the pole right sharp, then Marse Ike start to gig around with the pole, and he kinder laugh to hisself, cause he knowed he done found Jim. Bout that time Jim poke he head up and say: "This here me," and everybody holler. Then he ax em, please, for God's sake, don't let them dogs git him. They told him to come on out.

You see, Jim belonged to Miss Mary Lee, Mr. John Lee's ma, and his pa was kilt in the war, so Mr. Beesley was looking out for her. Well, they took Jim outer there, and Mr. Beesley whipped him a little and told him: "Jim, you put up a pretty good fight, and I's gwine to give you a start for a run with the dogs."

Jim took out toward Miss Mary's, and Mr. Beesley held Old Brown as long as he could. They caught Jim and bit him right smart. You see, they had to let em bite him a little to satisfy the dogs. Jim could have made it, cept he was all hot and wore out.

That's about all I knows, cept us belonged to Marse Ike Horn, and first us belonged to Mr. Price Williams, what run the hotel in Livingston. He took my grandma to Mobile, then he died. Us ma belonged to they two chillun, Miss Nancy Gulley, Mr. Jake's wife, and Miss Burt Blakeney. Marse Ike Horn was they uncle, and us all come round to him, and us been here ever since. My mammy was Ann Campbell, and my pappy was John Horn, and us ain't never had no trouble with nobody bout nothing.

One time Marse Ike slip up on a heap of niggers at a frolic twixt Sumterville and Livingston and put a end to the frolic. The niggers having a big dance, and Marse Ike and the patterollers having a big run, said they wanted to have some fun, and they did. Said he eased up on em with a white sheet round him and a big bresh in he hand, and somehow or another, they didn't see him 'til he spoke. Then he holler "By God, I'm bird-blinding," and he say them niggers tore down them dirt chimleys and run through that house. He say he ain't never heared such a fuss in a corn-field in his born days. What he mean bout "bird-blinding"? When you goes in a canebrake it so thick, you takes a light to shine the bird's eyes and blind em, then you kin ketch em. That what he call bird-blinding. Yessum, Marse Ike in that, too. He couldn't stand for em to have no fun without he in it.

I's too sleepy to sing you no song, but one I laks is this. It suits me now in my old age:

My lates sun is sinking fas',
My race is nearly run,
My strongs' trial now is pas',
My triump' jes begun.

You come back and I'll sing the rest. I's got to see bout things now.

Massa Had a Way
of Looking at You

Isam Morgan
MOBILE

Mistress, I was bawn in 1853, 'cording to Old Miss's
Bible, near Lotts Landing on the Alabama River. Mr. James
Morgan was my massa, and his wife, Miss Delia, was my
mistress. My mammy's name was Ann Morgan, and as for
my pappy, I done forgot his'n. I was raised right there in
the white folks' house, and I had my own special place to
sleep. I was the house boy, and when I growed older I drive
Mistress around in the carriage.

Us niggers lived in sho-nuff style. Us had our regular
quarters whar us lived in white log cabins chinked with

mud, and the slaves had built-in beds and a big open fire-place where they cooked. Us had plenty somep'n t'eat. All us had to do was to ask for it, and the massa done the rest. Our rations was give out to us every Sat'day. Some of the best food us ever had was possum and taters. Us'd go out at night with a big sack and a pack of hounds, and twarn't long before we done treed a possum. After we treed him, the dogs would stand round the tree and bark. Iffen the tree was small, us could shake him out. Iffen it was big, one of the niggers hadta climb up it and git old Mr. Possum.

Funny thing about possums; the bigger they is seem lak the littler the tree they picks to go up. It is sho-nuff fun, though, to go a-trailing through the woods after a possum or coon. The coon'll give you the best chase, but he ain't no good eatin' lak the possum. I seen a coon one time when he was cornered bite the tip of a hound's nose off.

Massa Morgan sold wood to the steamboats, and us slaves hadta cut the wood and split it up into smaller pieces. Any time a slave worked overtime or cut mo' wood than he s'pose to, Massa pay him money for it, cause whenever one of us slaves seen somep'n we lak, we did jes lak the white folks does now. Us bought it.

Massa never whupped none of his slaves. He jes told us what to do and iffen we didn't do it, he'd call us to him, and he would say in his sorta way: "Nigger! How many mo' times is I gotta tell you to do lak you told?" That's all he would say, and believe me, Mistress, he had a way of lookin' at you that made you jump. When he bought a new slave that wasn't use to doin' what he was told, 'twarn't long before Massa had him in line.

None of our slaves ever tried to run away. They all knowed they was well off. We didn't have no overseer but once. He was a mean un, too. He tried to fight and whup us slaves, and one night six big nigger men jumped on him and scairt him most to death. After that the massa wouldn't never had no mo' overseers. He tended to that business hisself.

What we do after we finished work? Us was so tired us wouldn't lie down two minutes 'fore us was 'sleep. On some moonlight nights us was 'lowed to pick the cotton. Then us'd git a little res' the next day.

Massa and his family used brass lamps and candles for light, and a few of us slaves had brass lamps, too, but most of the niggers used torch lights.

Some of the plantations had a calaboose whar they put the slaves that wouldn't behave. This calaboose was built of logs fastened together with stout ropes and sunk into the ground, but Massa didn't need no calaboose to make his niggers behave.

Yassum, us had rememdies for ailments. We used wild hoarhound tea for the chills and fever, and sweet gum turpentine, and mutton suet. They was all good uns, too. But shucks! Warn't nothin' much ever the matter with us niggers.

We used rock and cotton to start the fires on the plantation, and Massa had a flintlock rifle, too.

The slaves had their own special graveyard, and us'd make the coffins right on the place there. When someone die, he was taken in a ox cart to the grave, with all the slaves a-walkin' 'long behind the cart singin' the spirituals.

Our clothes was made mostly outen osnaburg wove on the plantation. We had wool clothes for the wintertime that was carded on the place. We had shoes made by our own cobbler and tanned on the plantation. We called these brogans.

After the Surrender, the Yankees camped near our place and bought eggs from us. They offered me a hoss if-fen I would go nawth with them, but I jes couldn't leave Massa, even though I did wanted that hoss mighty bad. I was twenty-one years old when Massa came to me one day and say: "Isam, you is a grown man now. You is got to boss your own business. It's up to you to find work. I can't keep you no longer. Good luck, Isam. You has been a good nigger, and you is gonna make somebody a good worker."

After I left Massa I worked at diff'ent jobs, such as: loader, roustabout on diff'ent steamboats, and cotton picker. I worked on the *Lay Boyd*, *Lula D.*, and the *Gardner*. One of the ol' songs sang on the boats went somep'n lak this:

The *John T. Moore*
The *Lula D.*
And all them boats is mine
If you can't ship on the *Lula D.*,
You ain't no man o' mine.

I been married three times, Mistress, and Lawd, chile, I done forgot the name of my fust wife. I guess she still livin' somewhere cause she was too mean to die. My second wife was named Dora, and she is daid. I got a wife now named Lily. She purty good.

Yes, ma'am, you can take my picture, but lemme git my hat, cause I ain't got no hair on my head, and I looks better with a hat. I's got to be fixed up stylish.

Peter Had No Keys
Ceptin' His'n

George Young
LIVINGSTON

I was born on what was knowed as the Chapman Place, five miles nor'west of Livingston, on August 10, 1846. I had five brothers (Anderson, Harrison, William, Henry, and Sam) and three sisters (Phoebe, Frances, and Amelia). My mother's name was Mary Ann Chapman, and my father's name was Sam Young, but he belonged to Mr. Chapman. Us all belonged to Governor Reuben Chapman of Alabama.

The overseer's name was Mr. John Smith, and another's name was Mr. Lawler. He was there the year I was born, and they called hit "Lawler Year." Both of em was mean, but Lawler, I hear tell, was the meanest.

They had over three hundred slaves, cause they had three plantations—one at Godke, one at Huntsville, and this here one. I can't say Marse Chapman wasn't good to us, cause he was all the time in Huntsville and jes come now and then and bring his family to see bout things. But the overseers was sho' mean.

I seed slaves plenty times with iron bands round they ankles and a hole in the band and a iron rod fasten to hit what went up the outside of they leg to the waist and fasten to another iron band round the waist. This here was to keep em from bendin' they legs and runnin' away. They call hit "puttin' the stiff knee on you," and hit sho' made em stiff! Sometimes, that made em sick, too, cause they had them iron bands so tight round the ankles that when they took em off live things was under em, and that's what give em fever, they say. Us had to go out in the woods and git May-apple root and mullein weed and all such to boil for to cure the fever. Miss, whar was the Lord in them days? Whut was He doin'?

But some of em runned away, anyhow. My brother, Harrison, was one, and they set the "nigger dogs" on him lak foxhounds run a fox today. They didn't run him down 'til bout night but finally they cotched him, and the hunters fetched him to the door and say: "Mary Ann, here Harrison." They then turned the dogs loose on him again, and such a screamin' you never heared. He was all bloody, and Mammy was a-hollering, "Save him, Lord. Save my chile, and don't let them dogs eat him up." Mr. Lawler said, "The Lord ain't got nothin' do with this here," and hit sho' look lak He didn't, cause them dogs nigh bout chewed Harrison up. Them was hard times, sho'.

They didn't learn us nothin' and didn't 'low us to learn nothin'. Iffen they ketch us learnin' to read and write, they cut us hand off. They didn't 'low us to go to church, neither. Sometimes us slip off and have a little prayer meetin' by us selves in a old house with a dirt floor. They'd git happy and shout and couldn't nobody hear em, cause they didn't make no fuss on the dirt floor, and one stand in the door and watch. Some folks put they head in the washpot to pray, and pray easy, and somebody be watchin' for the overseer. Us git whupped fer everything iffen hit was public knowed.

Us wasn't 'lowed to visit nobody from place to place, and I seed Jim Dawson stobbed [staked] out with four stobs. They laid him down on his belly and stretch his hands out on both sides and tie one to one stob, and one to the other. Both his feet was stretch out and tied to them stobs. Then they whupped him with a whole board whut you kiver a house with. The darkies had to go there in the night and take him up in a sheet and carry him home, but he didn't die. He was 'cused of gwine over to the neighbor's plantation at night. Nine o'clock was the last hour us had to be closed in. Head man come out and holler, "Oh, yes! Oh, yes! Ev'ybody in and doors locked." And iffen you wasn't, you got whupped.

Wasn't nobody 'lowed to court. Us jes taken up together and go ahead, and that thing wasn't fixed 'til after Surrender.

The patterollers come from different places, and the Tank'sleys, the Potts, the Cock'ells, and the Greg'rys was neighbors. I may of went to they house and they claim to protect me playing with they little nigger chillun, but iffen the patterollers ketch me, they claim they wasn't 'sponsible. One day, they took out after me and I come right here in Livingston, but I was gwine run away anyhow, cause I had seed old Uncle Thornton that morning. See, I was the calf nurser and soon as I left the house I met him, and here come the overseer, Mr. Smith. He sent after me and he said, "I seed six niggers in the woods what run away," and asked did I see Old Man Thornton. I said, "No, I ain't seed nobody." He said, "Never mind, I make you tell a better tale 'n that in the mawnin'." So when I went with the slop to them calves I got to thinking bout that whupping so I come right here.

Mr. Norville had a woodshop right across the road there by the white folks' Baptist Church and I hid in the back of hit that night. But they found me and took me back. Then they stop me from calf nursing and put me in the field under the head man. I was glad of that, cause I wanted to be with the other hands, but when I found out how 'twas, I wanted to be back. Hit was a harder task then when I was nursing calves and keeping em from breaking in the field and eating up the crop.

I was a good hand and obeyed the owners and the head man and never had no excuse bout work. I went one time to Bennet's Station, ten miles below here, with jes seven more niggers from Chapman place, and us drive over a thousand head of cattle to Atlanta, Georgia, and never had no trouble. I was easy pleased. Give me a piece of candy and I'd lick hit 'til my mouth was sore. I reckon hit was all right, but I don't know. All the nations couldn't rule. Jes lak hit is now, the strongest people must rule.

After Surrender, they took a darkie for the probate jedge, but that nigger didn't know nothin' and he couldn't rule. So then they took a white man named Sanders, and he done all right. We was under hard taskmasters and I'm glad they set me free, cause I was under burden and bound. But ignerrancy can't rule, hit sho' can't. We is darkies, and white folks ought to be favorable. Some speaks better words'n others, but ev'ybody ain't got the same heart, and that's all I knows.

No'm, I don't know nothin' bout no spirits either, but Christ 'peared to the 'postles, didn't He, after He been dead? And I's seed folks done been dead jes as natural in the day as you is now. One day me and my wife was pickin' cotton right out yonder on Mr. White's place, and I looked up and seed a man all dressed in black, with a white shirt bosom, his hat a-sitting on one side, ridin' a black hoss.

I stoop down to pick some cotton, then look up and he was gone. I said to my wife, I said, "Glover, wonder whar that man went what was ridin' long yonder on that pacin' hoss?"

Glover say, "What pacin' hoss and what man?"

I said, "He was comin' down that bank by that ditch. They ain't no bridge there, and no hoss could jump hit."

Glover said, "Well, I'm gwine in the house cause I don't feel lak pickin' cotton today."

But I ain't skeered of em. I gets out the path plenty

times to let em by, and iffen you kin see em, walk round em. Iffen you can't see em, then they'll walk round you. Iffen they gets too plentiful, I jes hangs a hoss-shoe upside down over the door, and don't have no more trouble. But ev'ybody oughter have that kinder mind, to honor God. He 'peared to the 'ciples after He died, and He said also, "Peter, I'll give you the keys to the kingdom." But Peter didn't have nobody's keys ceptin' his'n. Don't you know iffen he'd of give Peter all them keys, they's a heap of folks Peter gwineter keep out of there jes for spite? God ain't gwineter do nothing that foolish. Peter didn't have nobody's keys ceptin' Peter's!

These Uppity Niggers

Mary Rice
EUFAULA

Honey, I lived in the quarter. I was a field nigger, but when I was a li'l gal, I helped around the milk-house, churning, washing the pails and the lak, and then give all the little niggers milk.

Massa Cullen and Mistress Mary Jane was the best marster and mistress in the world. Once when I was awful sick, Mistress Mary Jane had me brung in the Big House and put me in a room on the other side of the kitchen so she could take care of me herself cause it was a right fur piece to the quarter and I had to be nursed day and night.

I was jes as happy being a field hand as I would'er been

at the Big House, maybe more so. The field hands had a long spell when the crops was laid by in the summer and that's when Massa Cullen 'lowed us to "jubilate" [several work-free days of celebration]. I was happy all the time in slavery days, but there ain't much to git happy over now, 'cepting I's living—thank the Lawd. Massa Cullen was a rich man, and owned all the world from Chestnut Hill to the rivers, and us always had everything us needed.

Niggers these days ain't never knowed what good times is. Mebbe that's why they ain't no 'count. And they is so uppity, too, calling theyselves "colored folks" and having gold teeth. They says the more gold teeths they has, the higher up in the church they sets. Huh!

What I Keer About Bein' Free?

Nannie Bradfield
UNIONTOWN

I was bout twelve year old in May when 'mancipation come. My pa and ma belonged to Mars James and Miss Rebecca Chambers. They plantation was jes on the edge of town, and that's where I was born. Mars James's son, William, was in the war and Old Miss would send me to town where all the soldiers' tents was, to tote somep'n good to eat to them. I don't 'member much bout the war cept the tents and the bombshells shooting.

I was little and couldn't do much, but I waited on Miss Lizbeth, my young miss, and waited on table, toted battie cakes and such-like. I don't know nothing bout the pat-terollers or the Ku Kluxers, but I know all bout the conjure doctors. They sho' can fix you. They can take yo' garter or yo' stocking-top and drop it in running water and make you run the rest of yo' life. You'll be in a hurry all the time, and if they gits holt of a piece of the seat of yo' drawers they sprinkles a little conjure powder on it and burns it. Then you can't never set down in no peace. You jes like you setting on a coal of fish 'til you git somebody to take the spell offen you.

What I keer about bein' free? Didn't Old Marster give us plenty good somep'n to eat and clothes to wear? I stayed on the plantation 'til I married. My old miss give me a brown dress and hat. Well, that dress put me in the country; if you marry in brown you'll live in the country.

I ain't got no chillun, but Bradfield had plenty of em. I was his fourth wife. He died bout three years ago and he done well to live that long with all them womens to nag him. The Bible say it's better to climb on top of the house and set, than to live inside with a nagging woman.

I Loved to Pick That Box

George Dillard
EUTAW

Honey, there was a dance every Sat'day night, and all the niggers nigh bout broke they legs a-dancing.

I was right spry, but I was at my best in the job of pickin' the banjo. I sho' did love to pick that box while the other niggers danced away.

Us had plenty to eat. The food was cooked in Old Mistress's kitchen and sent to the field on a big cart. I 'member that a bell would ring for us to get up, and we would work as long as it was daylight.

Old Massa had a church right on the plantation for

us niggers. Many's the time I danced late in the night and then had to git up and go to church with the rest. All of us had to go. A white man would preach, but I always enjoyed the singin' most of all.

Ghosts is all around, but they don't follow me. I's not 'fraid of em, but I knows plenty of niggers that'll run if a ghost so much as brushes by em.

The white folks helped me to git myself a woman and then to git married to her. I had a nice wedding. It was a bunch of them [children he had], but I loved every one [24 total].

I Would Talk
a Lot for a Dime

Rufus Dirt
BIRMINGHAM

Boss, if you wants, I'll talk all day fo' that much money [a dime the interviewer offered him]. I's been here fo' a long time and I knows plenty to talk bout.

I don' rightly know just how old I is. I was a driver [Negro boss of other slaves] during slavery and I reckons I was about twenty something. I don' remember nothin' in particular that caused me to get that drivin' job, ceptin' hard work, but I knows that I was proud of it cause I didn' have to work so hard no more. And it sorta made the other niggers look up to me, and you knows us niggers, Boss. Nothin' makes us happier than to strut in front of other niggers.

We jes moved one crop after the other 'til lay-by time come and then we'd start in on winter work. We done jes bout the same as all the other plantations.

My massa's name was Digby, and we live at Tuscaloosa before the war. That war, white folks, them was some scary times. The nigger women was a-feared to breathe out loud come night. In the daytime, they didn't work much cause they was always lookin' fo' the Yankees. They didn't come by so much cause after the first few times there wasn't no reason to come by. They had done et up everything and toted off what they didn't et. They took all Massa's stock, burned down the smokehouse after they took the meat out, and they burned the barn, and we all think every time that they goin' to burn the house down, but they musta forgot to do that.

When the war was finally over and I was free, my family went to Vicksburg, Mississippi, where we made a livin' in first one way and then the other. I don' know how long we stayed there, but I was livin' in Birmingham when there wasn't nothin' much here a'tall [Birmingham was founded after the war, in 1871]. I watched all the big buildin's round here go up, and I seed them build all the big plants and I's still watchin', but I still don' know how to tell folks where places is, cause I don't know how to read numbers. I goes anywhere I wants to go and I don't ever get lost, but jes the same, I can't tell nobody where I am. I don't even know where we is standing talking like this right now. And, Boss, I ain't beggin' cause I's too lazy to work. I's worked plenty in my time 'til I cripples this arm in the mines and before my eyes got so bad.

Cabins As Far
As You Could See

Katherine Eppes
UNIONTOWN

Sho' honey, I can tell you more'n anything you want
to know bout the big fight, cause I been here a long time.
They ain't many left to tell bout them days. My mammy
and pappy was Peter and Emma Lines, and us all belong to
Marse Frank and Miss Sarah Lines. I was born on the plantation five mile below Faunsdale bout 1850, so they tells me.

I is right old but, thank Gawd, I still got my teefies and
my hair. I sees pretty good, too, but I's so heavy I ain't able
to toe myself round as pert as I useta.

It was different back in them days when I belonged to
rich white folks. They had plenty of niggers, and they was

log cabins in the quarters just as far as your eyes could see. Marse Frank and Miss Sarah was good to the black folks, too. Their son, Young Marse Frank, fought in the big war.

After the war I stayed on the Lines place 'til after I married, and Old Miss gave me my weddin' dress and a long veil down to my foots.

When us was chillun in the quarters we did a mighty lot of playin'. Us useta play "Sail away, Rauley" a whole lot. Us would hold hands and go round in a ring, gittin' faster and faster, and them what fell down was outa the game.

My mammy worked in the Big House, spinnin' and nursin' the white chillun. All of them called her "Mammy." I remembers one thing just like it was yesterday. Miss Sarah went to Demopolis to visit with her sister, and whilst she were gone, the overseer, what go by the name of Allen, whupped my mammy cross her back until the blood runned out.

When Miss Sarah comed back and found it out, she was the maddest white lady I ever seed. She sent for the overseer, and she say: "Allen, what you mean by whupping Mammy? You know I don't allow you to touch my house servants." She jerk her dress down and stand there lookin' like a soldier with her white shoulders shinin' like a snow bank, and she say: "I rather see them marks on my own shoulders than to see em on Mammy's. They wouldn't hurt me no worse." Then she say: "Allen, take your family and get offen my place. Don't you let sundown catch you here." So he left. He wasn't nothing but white trash nohow.

Honey, is you a Christian? I hopes you is, because you

is too fine lookin' for to go to Hell. I belongs to the Baptist Church, and they calls me Ma Eppes because I's the mother of the church. I loves to sing the gospel hymns:

I am a soldier of the cross,
A follower of the lam'.
I'm not afeard to own His name,
Nor to defend His cause.
I want you to come,
I want you to come,
I want you to come,
And be saved.

In Slavery Time

Martha Bradley
MOUNT MEIGS

Our marster was sho' good to all his niggers. Us allus had plenty to eat and plenty to wear, but the days now is hard. If white folks give you a nickel or dime to git you somep'n to eat you has to write everything down in a book before you can git it. I allus worked in the field, had to carry big logs, had straps on my arms and them logs was put in the strap and hauled to a pile. One morning hit was raining, and I didn't wanna go to the field, but the overseer he come and got me and started whupping me. I jumped on him and bit and kicked him 'til he lemme go. I didn't know no better then. I didn't know he was the one to do that.

But Marster Lucas give us big times on Christmas and

July. [Lucas was a physician and a member of a prominent early family in east central Alabama. A "ball" was staged at Lucas Tavern for the Marquis de Lafayette on his visit to Alabama in 1824.] Us would have big dinners and all the lemonade us could drink. The dinner'd be spread out on the ground, and all the niggers would stand round and eat all they wanted. What was left we'd take it to our cabins. Nancy Lucas was the cook for everybody. Well, she'd sho' cook good cake and had plenty of em, but she wouldn't lak to cut them cakes often. She keep em in a safe. One day I got to that safe and I seed some and I wanted hit so bad 'til I jes had to have some. Nancy say to me, "Martha, did you cut that cake?" I say, "No sir! That knife just flew round by itself and cut that cake."

One day I was working in the field, and the overseer he come round and say somep'n to me had no business say. I took my hoe and knocked him plumb down. I knowed I's done somep'n bad so I run to the bushes. Marster Lucas come and got me and started whupping me. I say to Marster Lucas what that overseer say to me and Marster Lucas didn't hit me no more. Marster Lucas wouldn't let nobody run over his niggers.

There was plenty white folks that was sho' bad to the niggers, and 'specially them overseers. A nigger what lived on the plantation j'ining ours shot and killed an overseer; then he run away. He come to the river and seed a white man on the other side and say, "Come and git me." Well, when they got him they found out what he'd done and was gwine to burn him alive. Judge Clements, the man that keep law and order, say he wouldn't burn a dog alive, so he left. But they sho' burn that nigger alive for I seed him after he was burned up.

We'd go to meeting to the Antioch Church some Sundays. Us'd go to the house and git a pass. When us'd pass by the patterollers, us jes hold up our pass and then us'd go on. [In the church] there was a 'viding twixt the niggers and the white folks. The white preacher'd preach, then the colored man. Us'd stay at church most all day. When we didn't go to church, we'd git together in the quarters and have preaching and singing amongst ourselves.

In cotton-picking time us'd stay in the field 'til way after dark and us'd pick by candlelight and then carry hit and put hit on the scaffold. In the wintertime us'd quilt; jes go from one house to another in the quarter. Us'd weave all our everyday clothes, but Marster Lucas'd go to Mobile every July and Christmas and git our Sunday clothes. Git us dresses and shoes, and we'd sho' be proud of em.

In slavery time they doctored the sick folks different from what they does now. I seed a man so sick they had to put medicine down his throat lak he was a horse. That man got well and sho' lived to turn a key in the jail. If hit was in these days, that man would be carried to the hospital and cut open lak a hawg.

There was a slave what lived in Macon County. He run away and when he was cotched they dug a hole in the ground and put him cross hit and beat him nigh to death.

Ole Joe Had Real 'Ligion

Walter Calloway
BIRMINGHAM

Come in, white folks. You ain't no doctor, is you? For the last twenty-five years I been keeping right on, working for the city in the street department. Bout two months ago this misery attacked me and don't 'pear lak nothing them doctors gives me do no good. The preacher he come to see me this morning, and he say he know a white gentleman doctor what he gwine to send to see me. I wants to git well agin powerful bad, but maybe I done live long nough and my time bout come.

I was born in Richmond, Virginny, in 1848. Before I was old enough to 'member much, my mammy with me and my older brother was sold to Marse John Calloway at

Snowdoun in Montgomery County, ten miles south of the town of Montgomery.

Marse John had a big plantation and lots of slaves. They treated us purty good but we had to work hard. Time I was ten years old I was making a regular hand hind the plow. Marse John good nough to us and we git plenty to eat, but he had a overseer named Green Bush what sho' whup us iffen we don't do to suit him. He mighty rough with us, but he didn't do the whupping hisself. He had a big black boy name Mose, mean as the devil and strong as a ox, and the overseer let him do all the whupping. He could sho' lay on that rawhide lash. He whupped a nigger gal bout thirteen years old so hard she nearly die, and allus afterwards she have spells of fits or somep'n. That make Marse John powerful mad, so he run that overseer off the place, and Mose didn't do no mo' whupping.

Same time Marse John buy Mammy and us boys, he buy a black man name Joe. He a preacher and the marster let the slaves build a bresh arbor in the pecan grove over in the big pasture. When the weather wasn't too cold all the slaves was allowed to meet there on Sunday for preaching.

Ole Joe do purty good. I speck he had mo' 'ligion than some of the high-falutin' niggers pretending to preach nowadays. The white folks' church, hit at Hope Hull over on the stage road, and sometimes they fetch their preacher to the plantation to preach to the slaves. But they'd ruther hear Joe.

We didn't git no schooling cepting before we got big nough to work in the field we go long to school with the white chillun to take care of em. They show us pictures and tell us all they can, but it don't 'mount to much.

When the war started most all I know bout it was all the white mens go to Montgomery and join the army. My brother, he bout fifteen year old, so he go long with the ration wagon to Montgomery mos' every week. One day he comes back from Montgomery, and he say, "Hell done broke loose in Georgia." He couldn't tell us much bout what done happen, but the slaves get all excited cause they didn't know what to expect. Purty soon we find out that some of the big mens call a meeting at the capitol on Goat Hill in Montgomery. They 'lected Mister Jeff Davis president and done busted the United States wide open.

After that there warn't much happen on the plantation cepting gangs of soldiers passing through gwine off to the war. Then bout every so often a squad of Confederate soldiers would come to the neighborhood gathering up rations for General Lee's army, they say. That make it purty hard on both whites and blacks, taking off some of the best stock and running us low on grub.

But we was alright 'til one day somebody sent a runner saying the Yankees coming. Old Mistress tell me to hurry over to Mrs. Freeman's and tell em Wilson's Yankee raiders was on the way and coming like a harricane. I hop on a mule and go jes as fast as I can make him travel, but before I git back they done reach the plantation, smashing things coming and gwine.

They broke in the smokehouse and took all the hams and other rations. They find what they want and burn up the rest. Then they ransack the Big House looking for money and jewelry, and raise Cain with the womenfolks cause they didn't find what they wanted. Then they leave their old hosses and mules and take the best we got. After they done that, they burn the smokehouse, the barns, the cribs, and some other property. Then they skedaddle someplace else.

I warn't up there but I hear they burn up piles and piles of cotton and lots of steamboats at Montgomery and left the town jes bout ruint. 'Twarn't long after that they tell us we's free. But lawdy, Cap'n, we ain't never been what I calls free. Course Old Marster didn't own us no mo', and all the folks soon scatter all over, but iffen they all lak me they still have to work jes as hard, and sometimes have less than we useta have when we stay on Marse John's plantation.

Well, Cap'n, that's bout all I know. I feel that misery coming on me now. Will you please, suh, gimme a lift back in the house? I wish that white gentleman doctor come on, iffen he's coming.

White Hen Is
Heaps of Company

Ella Dilliard
MOBILE

In those days, people had to work to live, and they raised most everything they used, such as cattle, hogs, cotton, and foodstuff. Then the women spun the thread out of the cotton, and wove the cloth.

We never had any ice way back yonder. We had nice, old, open brick wells, and the water was just like ice. We would draw the water and put around the milk and butter in the dairy. It's a mystery to me how they make that ice, my goodness! I guess I need not worry my head about things, because I am not here for long. All my family is dead and gone now, and the only companion I have is this here old white hen. Her name is Mary. You see, I bought her last year to kill for Christmas, but I couldn't do it. She is so human, and you ought to see the eggs she lays. I even have a few to sell sometimes. I just keeps Mary in the room at night with me, and she is heaps of company for me.

Gittin' My Pension

Cheney Cross
EVERGREEN

During the war, I had done long pass my thirteenth birthday.

Lawd, honey, here 'tis past dinnertime, thank you jes the same. What makes me so late here now, I stopped by Miss Ella Northcutt's. She's my folks, too, you know, and she done made me eat all I can hold. No'm, honey, I can't eat no cabbage. Me and cabbage never has set horses together much, but I will thank you for the iced tea.

Honey, you don't mind if I rests my feets, does you? My white folks is spoiling me today. I'll be lookin' for it tomorrow, too, and I won't be gittin' it.

I told Mr. Henry I's comin'. And here I is! How'd

I come? I come on Mack and Charlie, that's how! Yes, ma'am! These two boys here, these here foots, they's Mack and Charlie. They's my whole 'pendence for gittin' about. Don't you worry none. Mr. Harry, he'll get me back home 'gainst dark come on.

I don't want no better folks than Mr. Harry and Miss Emma. I follow them good folks clean up to Muscle Shoals! Yes'm, I sho' did. At first, I told em I couldn't go nohow. But they pull down on me so hard, look like I couldn't help myself.

Yes ma'am! I ain't been home no time a-tall neither, 'til here come Mr. Harry back to Evergreen with his own self. Yes, Lawd! I can see him now, comin' up the big hardwood road, his head rared back, a-smoking a cigarette like a millioniare! Lawd, Lawd! Me nor Mr. Harry neither one ain't never gonna be contentious nowhere but right here. And that's the Gawd's truth!

Iffen Mr. Harry hadn't come on back here, I never woulda had no pension. That's the Gawd's truth, too. Nobody here didn't know my exact age, cause this wasn't originally my home. All them what did know close onto my age done died out, and I knows it. So when Mr. Harry put out to help me, I says in my heart, "Thank Gawd!"

I told Mr. Harry that iffen anybody in the world knowed my age, it was my young mistress, and I didn't know exactly where she at, but her papa was Captain Purifire [Purifoy]. Back yonder he was the madistra [magistrate] of our town, and he had all them lawin' books. I figured that my birthright would be down in one of them books. I knowed in reason that my mistress still got them books with her, cause there ain't be no burnings that I heard about. I knowed, too, that Mr. Harry was gonna find out where she was at.

I 'members Captain Purifire jes like a book. I does that! Now, course, when he come on in home from the war he didn't exactly favor hisself then, cause when I seed him coming round the house he look so ragged and ornery I took him for the old Bad Man hisself. I took out behind the smokehouse, and when I got a good look at him through the crack it look like I could recognize his favor, but I couldn't call his name to save my life. Lawd, honey! He's a sight! All growed over and bushy! You couldn't tell iffen he's a man or beast. I kept on lookin whilst he's coming around the corner, and then I heard him say, "Cheney, that you?" I's so happy, I jes melt down.

You see, it's like this. My foreparents, they was bought. My mistress and my daddy's mistress, too, was Miss Mary Fields, and my daddy was Henry Fields. Then the Carters bought my daddy from Miss Mary Fields. Well, they mix up and down like that, 'til now my young mistress, what use to be little Frances Purifire, she's married to Mr. Cunningham.

I was brung right in the house with my white folks. Yes'm, I slept on the little trundler bed what pushed up under the big bed during the day. I watched over them chillun day and night. I washed em, and fed em, and played with em. When she cry, my mistress say, "Cheney, go on and get that goat." Yes, Lawd! An that goat sho' did talk sweet to that baby. Jes like it was her own. She look at it and wag her tail so fast and say, "Ma-a-a-a-a!" Then she lay down on the floor whilst us holds her feets and lets the baby suck the milk. All the time that goat be's talkin', "Ma-a-a-a," til that baby got satchified.

When us chillun got took with any kind of sickness or diseases, us took azzifizzity [asafetida] and garlit [garlic]. You know, garlit what smells like onions. Then we wore some round us necks. That keep off [influenza].

These days it look like somep'n to eat don't taste like that we cook back yonder. The coffee us used had to be fresh ground, every day. And when it commence to boil, I put these here knees down on the floor before the fire and stir that coffee for the longest. Then my grandma, she hung that pot up on them pot hooks over the fire, and washed the meat, and drop it in. Time she done pick and overlook the greens and then wrinched [rinsed] em in spring water, the meat was boilin'. Then she take a great big mess of them fresh turnip greens and squash em down in that pot. They jes melt down and go to seasonin'.

Next thing I knowed, here come my mistress, and she say, "Now, Cheney, I wants some ponebread for dinner." Them hickory coals in that fireplace was all time ready and hot. They wouldn't be no fingerprints left on that pone when Cheney got through pattin' it out neither. Better not! Look like them chillun jes couldn't get nough of that hard cornbread.

Plenty of fancy cooking went on round that fireplace. But somehow the pot liquor and ponebread longside with the fresh buttermilk stirs my memory better'n anything.

All this good eatin' took place before the Yankees

raided us. It was then, too, that my mistress took me down to the spring back of the house. Down there it was a hollow tree stump, taller'n you is. She tell me to climb up to the top of that hollow tree. Then she hand me a big heavy bundle, all wrapped up and tied tight. It sho' was heavy! Then she say, "Drop it in, Cheney." I didn't know then what she's up to, but that was the silver and jewelry she's hidin'.

Yes, honey, I 'members that Yankee raid like it was jes yestiddy. I's settin' there in the loom room, and Mr. Thad Watts's l'il gal, Louise, she's standin' at the winder. She say, "O-o-o-h! Nanny! Jes look down yonder!"

"Baby, what is that?" I says.

"Them's the Yankees comin'!"

"Gawd help us!" I says, and before I can catch my breath, the place is covered. You couldn't stir em up with a stick. Feets sounded like mutterin' thunder. Them [bayonets] stick up like they jes sittin' on the mouth of they guns. They swords hangin' on they sides singin' a tune whilst they walk. A chicken better not pass by. Iffen he do, off come his head.

When they pass on by me, they pretty near shook me outta my skin. "Where's the mens?" they say and shake me up. "Where's the arms?" they shake me 'til my eyeballs loosen up. "Where's the silver?" Lawd! Was my teefs droppin' out? They didn't give me the time to catch my breath. All the time, Miss Mary jes look em in the eye and say nothin'.

They took them Enfield rifles, half as long as that door, and bust in the smokehouse window. They jack me up off my feet and drag me up the ladder and say, "Git that meat out." I kept on throwin' out Miss Mary's hams and sausages, 'til they holler "stop." I come backing down that ladder like a squirrel, and I ain't stop backing 'til I reach Miss Mary.

Yes, Lawd! Them Yankees loaded up a wagon full of meat and took the whole barrel of 'lasses. Takin' that 'lasses killed us chillun. Our main 'musement was making 'lasses candy. Then us cakewalk round it. Now that was all gone.

Look like them soldiers had to sharpen they swords on everything in sight. The big crepe mullen [myrtle] bush by the parlor window was blooming so pink and pretty, and they jes stood there and whack off them blooms like folks's heads droppin' to the groun'.

I seed the sergeant when he run his bayonet through Miss Mary's bestest feather bed and rip it slam open! With that, a wind blowed up and took them feathers every which way for Sunday. You couldn't see where you's at. The sergeant, he jes throwed his head back and laugh fit to kill hisself. Then first thing next, he done suck a feather down his windpipe. Lawd, honey, that white man sho' struggled. Them soldiers throwed water in his face. They sock 'im, and beat 'im, and roll 'im over, and all the time he's gettin limberer and bluer. Then they jack him up by his feets and stand him on his head. Then they pump him up and down. Then they shook him 'til he spit. Then he come to.

They didn't cut no mo' mattresses. And they didn't cut nothin' much up in the parlor, cause that's where the lieutenant and the sergeant slept. But when they left the next day, the whole place was strewed with mutilation.

I 'members well back there during the war how once a

month a big box, longer'n I is and wider, too, was took to our soldier boys on the battlefield. You never seed the like the sausages that went in that box, with cake, and chicken, and pies, and Lawd, the butter all rolled up in cornshucks to keep it fresh. Everybody from everywhere come to fix that box and help pile in the stuff. Then you hear em say, "Poor soldiers! Put it in here!" Then everything look sort of misty, and they heads droop over like. Then you see a mother's breast heave with her silent prayer.

Directly after the Surrender, the Ku Kluxes sho' was bad after the Yankees. They do all sorts of things to aggravate em. They's continual tying grapevines cross the road, to get em tangled up and make em trip and break they own necks. That was bad, too, cause them poor Yankees never suspicioned no better'n that them vines jes blowed down or somep'n.

Long bout then, too, seem like haunts and spirits was riding everything. They raided mostly round the graveyard. Lawd, honey, I ain't hankerin' after passing by no graveyards. Course, I knows I got to go in there someday, but they do make me feel lonesome and kind of jubus.

I 'members one night when I's walkin' down the big road with Bud, and he say, "Look! Didn't you see me give that road? That haunt done push me clean outa my place." Now let me tell you somep'n. Iffen you ain't never been close to a haunt, you don't know nothin'. I 'lowed he gwine follow me home. When I got there I shucked mustard seeds down on my floor. When you sprinkles em like that he can't get outta that room 'til he done count ever' last one of them seeds. Well, sir, the next mornin' all us could see was somep'n like a lump of jelly layin' there on the floor 'mongst them seeds. Like he done counted hisself to a pulp.

After that night, I puts a big sifter down at my door. You know haunts has to count every hole in that sifter before they can come through. Some folks puts the Bible down there, too. The poor spirit has to read every word of that book before he crosses over.

I reckon bout the terriblest thing ever happen to me was that big lookin' glass. The lookin' glass was all laid out in the top of my trunk, waitin' for my weddin' day. One night, I's standin' by the trunk with it wide open. I seed somep'n black before my eyes and then a screech owl lit in my window right in my face. I's so scared I sat right down in the middle of the lookin' glass. It bust in a million pieces. Mamma throwed up her hands and holler, "Git up from there, gal. You gonna have seven years of bad luck. Shoo that hootin' owl away before he dies in your tracks!" Then I swoons off. I feels them haunts gettin' ready to ride me clean down in my grave. Bout then somep'n keep sayin' to me, over and over, "Throw them pieces of lookin' glass in runnin' water." Then it say, "Burn your mammy's old shoe and the screech owl leave." After I done that, my mind was at rest.

Soon as my daddy hear em firin' off for the Surrender, he put out for the plantation where he first belong. He left me with my mistress at Pine Flat, but twasn't long 'til he come back to get me and carry me home with him. I hates to leave my mistress, and she didn't want to part from me. She say, "Stay here with me, and I'll give you school learnin'." She say to Captain Purifire, "You go buy my l'il nigger a book. Get one of them Blue Back Websters," she say, "so I can eddicate her to spell." Then my daddy say, "Her mamma told me not to come home without her, and she has to go with me."

I never will forget ridin' behin' my daddy on that mule in the night. Us left in such a hurry I didn' get none of my clothes hardly, and I ain't seed my mistress from that day to today.

The Overseer's Mean

Amy Chapman
LIVINGSTON

I was born on Governor Reuben Chapman's place five miles north of Livingston on May 14, 1843. My name is Amy Chapman. My mother was Clary Chapman, and my pappy was Bob Chapman. They both came from Virginny— my mammy from Petersburg, and my pappy from Richmond. They was driv' down to Alabamy like cattle when Marse Reuben bought em. He had a lot of slaves cause he had a heap of plantations, but him and his wife stay most of the time in Huntsville, and they had a heap of white overseers. I had plenty of chilluns but not as many as my mammy.

Who was my husband? Lawd, chile, I ain't never had

no special husband. I even forgets who was the pappy of some of these chilluns of mine.

Us had a mean overseer, and since Marse Reuben warn't never at home, them overseers useta treat us somep'n awful. One day Marse Reuben come home, and when he found out that the overseer was mean to the slaves he commence to give him a lecture, but when Miss Ferlicia took a hand in the business, she didn't stop at no lecture, she told that overseer this, "I hear you take my women and turn their clothes over their heads and whip em. Any man that's got a family and would do such a thing oughtta be 'shamed of hisself, and iffen Governor Chapman can't make you leave, I can, so you see that road there? Well, make tracks then."

And, Mistress, he left right then. He didn't wait for no coaxin'. He was the meanest overseer us ever had. He took my oldest brother and had him stretched out jes like you see Christ on the cross. Had him chained, and I sat down on the ground by him and cried all night like Mary and them done. That overseer was the first one that ever put me in the field, and he whupped me with the cat-o-nine-tails when I was stark naked.

Then there was another mean man who was always a-beating nigger women cause they wouldn't mind him.

Us weren't learned to read and write, but Mr. Jerry Brown's were. He owned a big plantation. Us didn't go to no nigger church, cause there weren't none. I was baptized in Jones Creek, and Dr. Edmonds, a white preacher, joined me to the Jones Creek Baptist Church long 'fore the war, and the song I liked best was a white folks' song. 'Twarn't no nigger song. It was like they sing it now, 'cept mo' lovely, Miss, mo' lovely.

Dark was the night,
Col' was the groun'
On which my Savior lay.
Blood in drops of sweat ran down
In agony he pray.

Lawd, move that bitter cup
If such thy sacred will.
If not content I'll drink it up
Whose pleasure I'll fulfill.

And another one us niggers useta sing was mighty pretty.

In evil long I took the light
And led by shame and fear
When a new object stopped my flight
And stopped my wild career.

I saw him hangin' on a tree
In agony and blood.
He fixed his languid eyes on me
As near his cross I stood.

Sho' never 'til my latter breath
Can I forget that look.

He seemed to change me with his death
Yet not a word he spoke.

My conscience felt and owned the guilt
And plunged me in despair.
I saw my sins his blood had spilt
And helped to nail him there.

Yessum, I could tell you things about slavery times that would make yo' blood boil, but they's too terrible. I jes tries to forget.

I could tell you about bein' run myself with them nigger dogs, but I ain't gwine to do it. I will tell you though bout a mean man who whupped a colored woman near bout to death. She got so mad at him that she took his baby chile what was playin' round the yard and throwed it in a pot of lye that she was usin' to wash with. His wife come a-hollering an run her arm down in the boiling lye to get the chile out, and she near bout burned her arms off, but it didn't do no good cause when she jerked the chile out he was dead.

One day I seed old Uncle TipToe all bent over a-comin' down the road an I ax him what ail him and he say, "I's been in the stocks and been beat 'til the blood come. Then Old Massa 'nointed my flesh with red pepper and turpentine and I's been most dead, but I is somewhat better now." Uncle TipToe belonged to the meanest old marster around here.

But, honey, I ain't never told nobody all this and ain't gwine tell you no mo'. Ride me home now, cause I's cripple;

a cow was the cause of it. She drug me round that new orchard what I planted last fall. She done run away with me. Mistress, I wished you would do me a favor and write my son in Texas and tell him that I say iffen he 'pects me to make him anymore of them star quilts, he better come on here an cover my house. The roof sho' does leak bad.

I Heard Lincoln
Set Us Free

Henry Cheatam
MARYSVILLE

My mammy's name was Emmeline Cheatam, and my pappy's was Sam Cheatam. I don't remember my grandpappy and grandmammy atall.

Us slaves lived in log cabins what was daubed with clay to keep the rain and wind out, and the chimneys was made of clay and sticks. The beds was homemade and nailed against the wall with legs on the outer side. The massa's house was built of logs, too, but it was much bigger'n the nigger cabins and set way out in front of ourn. After the massa was kilt [in the war], Old Miss had a nigger overseer and that the meanest devil that ever lived on the Lawd's green earth. I promised myself when I growed up that I was going to kill that nigger iffen it was the last thing I ever done. Lots of times I's seen him beat my mammy, and one day I seen him beat my auntie who was big with a chile, and that man dug a round hole in the ground and put her stomach in it, and beat and beat her for a half hour straight 'til the baby come out right there in the hole.

Why the mistress 'low such treatment? A heap of times Old Miss didn't know nothing bout it, and the slaves better not tell her, cause that overseer whup em iffen he finds out they done gone and told. Yassum, white folks, I's seed some terrible things in my time. When the slaves would try to run away, our overseer would put chains on their legs with big long spikes 'tween their feets, so they couldn't get away. Then I's seen great bunches of slaves put up on the block and sold just lak they was cows. Sometimes the chilluns would be separated from their maws and paws.

I come pretty near being took away from my maw. When the slaves was being divided, one of Old Miss's daughters was a-going to Texas and I was going to have to go when somebody hollered, "Freedom!" and I sho' was glad cause I could stay with my mammy now.

In those days us had plenty of good, plain food, such as pot liquor, greens, cornbread, taters, peas, pears, and at hog killing us had chittlin's, and pig jowls, and backbone. Then us would cotch possums at night when they come up in the cornfield. Us never seed no flour dough.

As for fishing, we never did none, cause we had to work

too hard. We worked from can to can't. Git up at sunrise, go to the field, and stay until dark. In the middle of the day they would send our somep'n to eat to the field with a barrel of water. But for breakfast and supper, us had to cook our own grub they give us.

Our clothes warn't many. Us chilluns wore a one-piece suit made outen osnaburg, and us would have to take that off at night, wash it, and put it back on the next day. As for shoes, chillun never had none. You see, white folks, I was just a chile, just big enough to tote water to the fields.

I 'members when the Yankees was a-coming through I holped to carry the horses to the woods, and hide the meat, and bury the valubles, cause them Yankees took whatever they wanted, and you better not say nothing neither, cause they had them long swords hanging on their sides.

In them days, the slaves done all the work and carried all the news. The marsters sont notes from one plantation to another, and when they wanted the niggers to come to the Big House they would blow an old cow horn. They had a certain number of blows for certain niggers—that is, the niggers that was something. They would also use this horn for possum and coon hunting at night. The li'l niggers at night went to the Big House to spin and weave. I's spun a many roll and carded a many bat of cotton. I's also made a many tallow candle by tying strings onto a long stick and dropping them down into molds filled with tallow.

I's hid many a night in the fence corners when I'd be going to git my mammy some 'bacco. The patterollers would be out looking for slaves that didn't have no pass from their overseer, and I'd hear them a-coming and I'd hide 'til they pass on, cause iffen they cotch me I sho gwine have a sound beating.

The owners always took care of us, and when us got sick they would git a doctor, and Old Miss was all right, but that overseer was a devil. He wouldn't 'low no meeting on the place. Sometimes us would slip down the hill and turn the wash pot bottom-upwards so the sound of our voices would go under the pot, and us'd have a singing and praying right there.

Most of the slaves could go sometimes to the white folks' church when they gits a pass from their massa, but that mean overseer always tried to keep us from going so's us couldn't learn nothing. He didn't want us to learn to read and write, neither.

Us didn't have nothing like matches 'til I was growed. Us used flint rocks and cotton to start the fires.

Us didn't have nothing but food and clothes. We didn't have no garden of our own, and there wasn't no celebrating, cepting at hog killing. That was the biggest day of the year.

On Sat'day afternoon we was allowed to play, but I can't 'member none of our games. Us jus played like all li'l niggers did then. At nighttime us just went to our cabins and went to bed, cause we warn't 'lowed to do no singing. Most of the singing was done in the fields.

Cornshucking time come when they wanted to git the seed corn for planting, and us would commence the shucking when it commence raining.

Us niggers never married and I don't 'member any big weddings of the white folks. But they buried folks then the same as they does now, in a box. They would bury the slaves same as they done the white folks, but us didn't even have no baptizing on count of that overseer. He didn't lak for us to git no religion. Course all slaves didn't have hard treatment lak us did, cause their overseer and marster warn't as mean as ours.

We didn't know nothing bout no hoodoo stuff in them days. They only had homemade medicines, that is unless they got sho' nuff powerful sick, and then they would go to see a doctor. Us used boneset tea made from a weed. Lawd, it was bitterer than quinine, and it were good for the chills and fever, and it would purge you, too. Us used life-everlasting tea for fever, and Jerusalem breshweed to git rid of worms.

I knows there is ghosts, cause when I was a little boy my mammy come in from the field and laid across the bed, and I was sitting in front of the fireplace, and a big something lak a cow without no head come in the door, and I commence to beat on it with my fists. Then my mammy say, "What matter with you, nigger?" Then that critter he walk right out the door. I looked outen the window and there it was a-going in Aunt Marfa's cabin. I never did see it no more. Then another time a white man died, and my mammy was staying with his sister, and this spirit lak an angel come to my mammy and told her to tell the white lady to read the Bible backwards three times, cause there was one talent 'tween her and Jesus. After that she were comforted. Another time, my pappy, Sam Cheatam, who was a wicked man, was a-sitting in front of the fire and a big brindle dog come to the door and started barking. My pappy say: "What in the Hell was that?" and snapped his fingers at the dog. The dog, he then dropped dead. Some folks say there ain't no such things as ghosts, but I say there is, cause there is good spirits and bad spirits.

Them was good old days, Mistress, even iffen us did have a hard time, and I don't know iffen it warn't better'n it is now. I has to almost go hongry, and I can't git no help from the government, cause I is over sixty-five years old. Fact is, I believe I druther be a-living back there than today cause us at least had plenty somep'n to eat and nothing to worry about. And as for beating, they beats folks now iffen they don't do right, so what's the difference?

I worked as long as I was able and didn't ask nobody for nothing, but now it's different cause I ain't able to do no work. I's tried to do right and ain't never been in but one fight in my life. I now belongs to the Corinthian Baptist Church, and I's trying to live so when the good Lawd calls I'll be ready to answer with a clean soul.

I's had two wives, but I was only a young nigger when I had the first un and had two chilluns by her, then I left her cause she warn't no count. That's been forty years ago, and I ain't never seen my chilluns in all them years. My second wife I got when I lived thirty miles below Birmingham, at the old Bank Mines. That's been thirty-five years ago and us is still together. Us ain't never had no chilluns.

I don't know nothing bout Abe Lincoln cepting they say he set us free, and I don't know nothing bout that neither.

Sometime an
Old Nigger Die

Allen Sims
LEE COUNTY

I 'members lots bout slavery times, cause I was right there. I don't 'member much bout the war, cause I was too little to know what war was, and the most I seed was when the Yankees come through and burnt up the Big House, the barns, the ginhouse, and took all Old Marster's hosses and mules, and kilt the milk cows for beef. They didn't leave us nothing to eat, and us lak to starve to death.

Our folks, the Simses, come from Virginny. My pappy and mammy was borned there. They names was Allen Sims and Kitty Sims. My old marster was Marse Jimmie Sims, and my old mistress was Miss Creasie. Some of Pappy and Mammy's chillun was borned in Virginny and some of em in Alabama. I was the baby chile, and I was borned right on this very place whar us is now. They had a whole passel of chillun. There was Chaney, Becky, Judy, Sam, Phoebe, King, Alex, Jordan, and Allen.

Us lived in a log house in the quarter, with a board roof and a big rock fireplace with a stick-and-dirt chimley. We had plenty wood, and could build jes as big fire as we need, if the weather was cold. Mammy, she cook ashcake in the fireplace, and it was the best bread I ever eat, better'n any this store-bought bread. You ain't never eat no ashcake? Look, Missy, you don't know what good bread is lak!

Old Marster was good to his niggers and all of em, big and little, had plenty to eat, and it warn't trash, neither. Us had ashcake, hoecake, ponebread, meat and gravy, peas, greens, roast'n ears [ears of corn], pot liquor, and sweet taters, Irish taters, and goobers—I 'pect Old Marster's niggers live better than lots of white folks lives now.

Aunt Mandy, what was too old to work, looked after all the little nigger chilluns whilst they mammies was working, and she whip us with a bresh, if we didn't mind her, but she fuss more than she whip, and it didn't hurt much, but us cry lak she killing us.

When us got sick, Old Mistress looked after us herself, and she give us oil, and turpentine, and lobelia, and if that didn't cure us, she sent for the doctor—the same doctor that come to see her own family. Sometime an old nigger die, and Old Marster and Old Mistress they cry jes lak us did. They put em in a coffin and bury em in the graveyard, with the white preacher there, and nobody didn't work none that day, after us come back from the graveyard.

Our beds was bunks in the corner of the room, nailed to the wall and jes one post out in the floor. The little chilluns slept crosswise the big bed, and it was plumb full in cold weather.

Our clothes was osnaburg, spun and weave right at home, and it sho' did last a long time. The little niggers jes wore a long shirt 'til they got big 'nough to work in the field, and us had red shoes made at the tanyard to wear in wintertime, but us foots was tough and us went barefooted most all the winter, too. Us played games, too, generally jumping the rope and base.

The grown niggers had good times Sat'day nights, with dances, suppers, and wrasslin'. The cornshuckings was the biggest time they had, cause the neighbors come, and they laughed and hollered nearly all night.

Old Marster and Old Mistress lived in a big two-story white house. They had ten chillun, five boys and five gals, and they all growed up and married off. The old carriage driver was named Clark, and he sho' was proud. The overseer was Tetter Roberson, and he was mean. He beat niggers a lot, and by and by Old Marster turned him off [the plantation]. He used to blow the horn way before day to git the niggers up, and he work em 'til smack dark.

After the Yankees burned up everything cept the cabins, us jes stayed right there with Old Marster when us freed.

Old Marster built a new house for him and Old Mistress, but it wasn't much better than our cabin, and they lived there 'til they died.

When I growed up, I married Laura Frazier, and us had a big wedding and a preacher, and didn't jump over no broom lak some niggers did. Us had jes two chillun that lived to be grown. They is Filmore and Mary Lou, and us ain't got no gran'chillun.

When I got grown, I joined the Baptist Church at Rough Neck, cause I felt I had done enough wrong, and I been a deacon forty year.

Mad Bout Somep'n
So They Had a War

John Smith

UNIONTOWN

I was born somewhere in North Carolina but I been
livin' round these parts bout ninety year. I don't 'member
much bout my mammy and pappy cause I was took away
from them by the speckerlaters when I was bout thirteen
year old. The speckerlaters raised niggers to sell. They would
feed em up and git em fat and slick and make money on
em. I was sold off the block in "Speckerlaters Grove" in
North Carolina. The fust day I was put up I didn't sold, but
the next day I brung a thousand dollars. Mr. Saddler Smith

from Selma bought me. They called him "Saddler" Smith cause he was in the saddle business and made saddles for the army. They fotch us down on boats. I 'member the song the men on the boat singed. Hit go like this:

Up and down the Mobile Ribbers,
Two speckerlaters for one po' l'il nigger.

My marster was the best in this country. He didn't had many niggers, but he sho' took good care of them what he did had. He didn't 'low nobody to hit em a lick. Sometimes when I would git cotch up within some devilment the white folks would say, "Whose nigger is you?" and I say, "Marse Saddler Smith." Then they look at each other and say kinder low, "Better not do nothin' to Old Smith's nigger. He'll raise the devil."

I didn't have no mistress. My marster was a [widower]. He raised me up workin' round the saddle shop. I ain't never liked to work nohow, but don't tell nobody that. I was bout twenty-seven year old when the war broke out. The old uns was called out fust and the young uns stayed home and practiced so they could shoot straight and kill a Yankee. Us practiced every Friday evenin'. Course I didn't know what they fightin' bout. I jes knowed they was mad bout somep'n. After a while Marster's son Jim joined the 'federate soldiers and I went with him to tote his knapsack, and such-like, and to look after him. That's when I got these here balls in my side and got a bullet in my leg, too. I was movin' the hosses to the back of the lines out the thick of the fight when, zip, a minie ball cotch me right in the shoulder.

I slept right by Marse Jim's side. Sometime after us done laid down and both of us be thinkin' bout home, Marse Jim say, "John, I lak to have some chicken." I don't say nothin' I jes ease up and pull my hat down over my eyes and slip out. After while I come back with a bunch o' chickens crost my shoulder. Nex' mornin' Marse Jim have nice brown chicken floatin' in gravy what I done cook for him. Us was fightin' on Blue Mountain when Marse Jim got kilt. I looked and looked for him but I never did find him. After I lost my marster I didn't belong to nobody and the Yankees was takin' everything anyhow, so they took me with them.

I took care of Gen'l Wilson's hoss. Gen'l Wilson was the head man in the Yankee army. But I didn't lak they ways much. He wanted his hoss kept spic and span. He would take his white pocket hankerchief and rub over the hoss and if it was dirty he had me whupped. I was with Gen'l Wilson when he took Selma 'gainst Gen'l Forrest and set fire to all them things. I drive the artillery wagon sometime. After the Surrender I was kinda puny with the balls in my side.

I drove the stagecoach twixt Selma and Montgomery. I 'member my stops. They was Selma, Benton, Lowndesboro, and Montgomery. I drive four hosses to it. There was a livery stable at Benton, and I changed hosses there.

I ain't never been married. Niggers didn't marry in them days. I jes took up with one likely gal after another. I ain't even married to the one I got now. I jes ain't gwine tie myself down. Iffen I's free, I's gwine to be free.

I wish I might be back in them days, cause I been seed the devil since I been free. After I was free I didn't had no marster to 'pend on and I was hongry a heap of times. I belong to the 'federate nation and always will belong to y'all, but I reckon it's jes as well we is free cause I don't believe the white folks now days would make good marsters.

Us Gwine Walk
Them Gold Streets

Theodore Fontaine Stewart
EUFAULA

The years are mighty long without Lottie. She done gone on to the promise; I knows she with Jesus. And us gwine to walk the golden streets together holdin' hands.

I knows I's well past the ninety mark, cause I was borned 'fore the war and was a right pert boy at the Surrender.

I 'members all bout them times, and the Lord know they was better times then we got now, for white or black. Nobody was hongry then, and peoples didn't git in the devilment they gits in now. Folks went to the church and behaved themselves in those days.

My old marster was the richest man in Georgy. I knows you has heard of Marse Theodore Fontaine. He had three big plantations and mo' niggers than he could count. He moved close to Florence, Alabama, and his three places was so big you couldn't see cross the littlest field.

Old Marster he live in a big house, bigger than any meetin' house in Eufala. He had a gang of fine horses, and when company was thar he had horse races on his own track. His horses could beat all the horses brought thar, and that's the direct truth.

Old Marster didn't go to war. He too old to go, so he stay home and make corn, and fodder, and oats, and send them to the soldiers what was killin' Yankees. One day the Yankees come along and burnt up everything on the place, cept the nigger cabins. They took all the horses and everything us had to eat.

Old Marster went off somewhere when they comes. I don't 'member where, and when he come back he had to live in one of the nigger cabins 'til he could build a house. But the new one wasn't big lak the old one.

My pappy was a field hand 'til one time Old Marster put him on a horse to ride in a race, and pappy beat the other horse so far Old Marster was tickled pink. He said a nigger what could ride lak that had no business in the field, so he made a stableboy outen pappy.

Old Marster didn't have no old mistress. He say he so big all the ladies look funny 'side of him. When company was there his sisters, Mistress Mary and Mistress Lucy, come and kept house; but they left when the company did.

My pappy was named Ed Stewart, cause Old Marster buy him from a Stewart. After the war they call pappy's chilluns Stewart; but us is Fontaines by right, bet yo' life on that.

Old Marster was good to the niggers, but his overseers was mean. Old Marster fired them after awhile and got some good overseers. He didn't 'low them to whip a nigger cept when he say, and he didn't say so much.

Chillun Was Mannerable

George Taylor
MOBILE

My grandfather's name was Mac Wilson, and my grand-mother's name was Ellen Wilson, and the old miss was Miss Mamie Herrin. All the colored folks' chillun called Mr. Herrin "Old Marster," and he sho' was a good marster, too. I 'members that after I got to be a big boy they put me in the fields choppin' cotton, but I never could pick cotton. I knows that my paw said I was too crazy bout girls, so he took me and made me plow.

Old Marster had a big place, I don't jes exactly knows how many acres they was, but I knows us had plenty of cotton, cause sometimes they would pick four or five bales a day. And then I knows durin' cotton time my paw hauled cotton all day long to the gin what was run by five or six mules.

Durin' the busy season on the plantation Old Marster had the older women cookin' and sendin' the dinner to the field. There was two big baskets, one to put the bread in, and the other basket to put the meat in. Every mornin' at three o'clock the women begun cookin' and each hand brought his own meat and bread to this cabin to be cooked. Every person's plate had their names on em. Everybody had to be up by daylight and ready to begin work. The men had to get up before daylight and harness the mules, and soon as light they was in the fields. There was two hundred and fifty head of colored people, excusing chillun. They would raise four, five, and six hundred bales of cotton a year. Us worked then, there warn't no walkin' bout then, not even on Sat'day afternoons, but I believes I'd lak it better than I does now, cause the chillun was taught to be mannerable then, but now they cuss if you say anything to them.

Us had a good place to stay. The old Marster's house was a big two-story house, and our cabins was built of boards and was in a row. Us didn't have no stoves, jes cooked out in the yard over a fire with stakes on each side of hit, with an iron bar across em to hang the pots on. Old Marster rationed out the food, and each man was 'lowed seven pounds of meat, the women was 'lowed six pounds, and five pounds for each child. They give us a peck of meal, five pounds of flour, and some molasses.

I never did eat at home with my folks, cause I nursed in the Big House, and every time that the white chillun eat, I had to eat, too. There was plenty of peach, walnut, and chestnut trees on the place, and us could eat all the nuts we wanted; and then the slaves had their own gardens if they wanted to.

Then I 'members how there was four men who put the hogs in the pens to fatten, sometimes they would put as many as a hundred or a hundred and fifty at a time. Then hit was their duty to tote feed from the fields to feed em.

When I think of that big smokehouse, my mouth jes waters. At hog-killin' time, there was certain men to kill, and certain ones to cut em up. There warn't never no special time to hog killin', jes when the old marster said do hit, we did hit.

You see was allus under his direction, cause if us wanted to go anywhere, us had to git a pass, even to church. The white folks had Methodist church, and the colored had the Baptist church.

I also 'members the time I was put up on the block to be sold, and when the man only offered five hundred dollars fer me, and Old Marster told me to git down, that I was the mos' valuable nigger he had, cause I was so strong, and could do so much work.

My maw was the weaver, and there was a woman named Assella who did the dyeing. My paw gathered the bark, such as red oak, elm, maple, and juniper bark, and dry hit and then grin' hit up. They also used borax, alum, and bluestone to set the dye. The women made the clothes out of this cloth that was woven on the place.

Us didn't have weddin's lak us do now. The way us married would be to go to the Big House, and Old Marster had us to jump over a broomstick, and then us was considered married. But there was one thing that us warn't 'lowed to do, and that was to abuse or cuss our wives, and you better not strike em, cause hit would be jes too bad.

You know, I's been here a long time. I 'members the remedies that they used in the old days. They used red-oak bark for fever and colds, and then there was horehound, and blacksnake root that the old marster put whiskey on. Old Marster made his own whiskey. And, oh yes, the calamus root growed in the woods whar they lived. I never seed them send to no store for medicine. I never heered of no hoodoo stuff, 'til I was grown, and another thing, folks didn't die off lak they do now. When anyone did die, they allus had a big funeral, and the men would sometimes hitch up a ox team or mule team, and as many as could git in would go. The coffins was homemade and stained. There was plenty of hands to dig the graves, too.

Folks is pretty much the same, if the white folks treat the niggers right, you couldn't get them to leave them. I 'members when the Yankees come through, I was standin' on the old marster's porch, and I seed them coming, and Marster got up on his crutch and go to the steps and invite them in, and believe me they come in, too. They jes natcherly tore up Old Marster's place—threw the furniture all round and broke heaps of hit. I knows before they got there Old Marster had my paw, and Jerry Lee, and Mac

Pouncey, and another man take four barrels of money and carry down to the spring and put hit in the spring, and I's tellin' you, you couldn't any more git near that spring than nothin', cause the quicksand made them barrels boil up, one at a time, and the way they had to git them barrels was to build a scaffold from the river, and let a line down and ketch around them barrels.

After we was freed, Old Marster come out in the yard and got in the middle of all of us, and told us that the ones that wants to stay with him, to stand on one side, and the udders to stand on the other side. So my paw got on the side with those who wanted to leave, and us left Old Marster and paddled down the river in a paddlin' boat to Belle's Landing.

As I's said before, I's been here a long time. I even 'members seeing Jeff Davis. I knows I ain't here for long, but I's ready, cause I's been fightin' for Jesus twenty-nine years, and I ain't tired of fightin' yet.

Hid Things
They Ain't Never Found

Elizabeth Thomas
Montgomery

I lived mighty fine in them days, I tell you. Mister Ben Martin Jones was my marster, and I was born on the Red Bridge Road. I was a house servant. All our clothes was made at the quarters. My mammy made mine and all I wanted, too. I useta hear my mammy say, the patterollers would git us if we done wrong but I didn't know nothin' bout patterollers, cause they wasn't none on our place. They whipped you, too, but my marster could control all his niggers so he didn't 'low none of em on our place.

I was twenty-one years old when the Yankees come but I didn't run and they didn't do nothin' to me, but folks was in such a hurry they hid things that ain't never been foun' yet. I liked meetin' on Sundays and sometime we never got outen church 'til daylight. I wants to live jes as long as Jesus say and when he say go, I's ready. At Christmastimes we always had good dinners and heaps o' company, plenty of it. My missus died and after that my mother raised Old Marster's chile, Tommy John, right along with me. Oh, them was happy days, I tell you.

I Warn't No
Common Slave

Mollie Tillman
UNIONTOWN

I kin recolleck bout slavery times, cause I was a big old gal then. I 'members when the 'mancipation come as if 'twas yesterday. Honey, I warn't no common everyday slave; I helped the white folks in the Big House. Mistress Lucy wouldn't let em take me to the field. Them was good days, chile, but since 'mancipation I has jes had to scuffle and work and do the best I can.

Marse Dan was a Baptist preacher, and he was a good man. He was a chaplain in the big war, and he didn't get hurt. He was a powerful important man and owned lots and lots of slaves—the plantation jes full of niggers. When the Yankees come, they was jes ruination to the plantation. They took all the mules and cows, then sent out and got all the chickens and eggs they could fin'. Eatin' was kind of slack with us after they left.

I was old 'nough to be castin' my eyes round at the young bucks, and there was a nigger what lived on the plantation j'inin' our'n what took a shine to me. I laked that boy fine, too.

He would come over to see me every time he git a chance. One night he 'low he gwineter ax his marster to buy me so's me and him could git married. Well, after that he didn' come no mo'.

I waited an I watched, but I didn' hear nuffine of that nigger. After 'while I got worried the patterollers done kotch him, or maybe he done foun' some gal he lak better than he do me. So I begin to 'quire bout him and found that his marster done sold him to a white man what took him way down yonder to Alabama.

Well, ma'am, I grieved for that nigger so that my heart was heavy in my breast. I knowed I never would see him no mo'. Soon after that, peace was 'clared and the niggers was free to go whar they pleased.

My folks stayed on with Marse Dan for a year, then they 'cided to go to Alabama and farm. We hit off to Alabama and I begin to go bout some with the young bucks. But somehow I couldn't git my mind off that other nigger.

Well, ma'am, one day at a big meetin' I runned up on

him. I was so happy I shouted all over that meetin' house. We jes took up whar we left off and 'fore long us got married.

The Court Jester

Stepney Underwood
LOWNDES COUNTY

Yassuh, I was a slave. I was ten year old when the war begin. My mammy belonged to the Johnstons, and my pappy was owned by the Underwoods. They lived next to each other on two big plantations in Lowndes County. They was good people, them Underwoods. They useta think I was funny as a little monkey. The massa useta laugh his head off at me, and when there was parties, the guests would always say: "Whar Stepney? We wants to see Stepney dance." I useta cut many a grand pigeon wing fur em.

One day after I finish my chores, I slip off and across

the line to see my mammy. When I was a-comin' through the woods, I met up with two patterollers. They stop me and say: "Nigger, who you belong to?"

"Massa Jim Johnston," I answers.

"What you a-doing out here, then?" they say, all the time a-slippin' a little closer so's to grab me.

I don't take time to give em no mo' answers cause I knowed that this meant a beatin'. I starts my legs a-flying, and I runs through the forest lak a scared rabbit with them patterollers right behin' me. My bare feets flew over them stones, and I jes hit the high spots in the groun'. I knowed them two mens didn't have no chance to kotch me, but this sho' meant a whuppin' when I got home.

But I didn't go home that night. I stay out in the woods and build me a little fire. I laid down under a sycamore tree a-trying to make up my mind to go and take that beatin'. I heared the panthers a-screaming a way off in the forest, and the wildcats a-howling, and how I wishes I coulda been with my mammy. Every now and then, I could see eyes a-shining in the darkness and rustlings in the bushes. Warn't no use of me a-crying cause I was a long way from home and there warn't no one could hear me. Everything seem to be agin' me. Far off across the ridge I heared a screech owl a-calling, and I knowed that meant death. I was glad I had my overalls on so's I could turn my pockets inside out'ards to stop him. After I done this, he sho' nough stopped. Then my left ear it commence to itching, and I knowed that someone was a-saying somethin' mean about me. Probably that overseer that was a-going to whup me when I got home. Soon I fell slap to sleep on a bed of moss. The next day I was awful hongry, and long bout the time the sun was a-comin' over the ridge, I heared some mens a-comin' through the bresh. It was the massa, the overseer, and some mo' mens. I runs toward the massa, and I calls as loud as I could: "Massa Jim, here I is."

He come up with an awful frown on his face, and the overseer, he had a big whup in his hand.

"You little burrhead nigger devil," the massa say, "I teach you ter run away from yo' place. Come on home. I's gwine give you a good breakfast and fix you up in some decent clothes. I's got visitors a-comin', and here you is out in the woods when I needs you to dance." Then the massa, he smile lak I ain't done nothin' wrong. "I guess you wants yo' mammy, you little lonesome pickaninny. Well, I s'pose I have to go over and buy 'er, you little devil, you—now git on home."

I Can't Read No Writin'

Emma Crockett

I belonged to Marse Bill Hawkins and Miss Betty. I lived on their plantation right over yonder. My mammy was called Cassie Hawkins, and my pappy was Alfred Jolly. I was Emma Jolly 'fore I married old Henry Crockett. Us had five chillun, and they two of em livin' in Birmingham—Fannie and Mary.

I lives here with my grandchild now on Mr. Bob Davis's place. Us gets enough to eat, I reckon, but it's tight, I tell you that!

I fell out t'other day and had a misery in my head ever

since. I wish I could read but I wasn't never larnt nothin' cepting after Surrender Miss Sallie Cotes she showed us how to read printin'. But I can't read no writin'.

All I know, 'twas bad times, and folks got whupped, but I can't say who was to blame. Some was good, and some was bad. I seed the patterollers, and after Surrender the Ku Kluxes they come then, but didn't never bother me. See, I wasn't so old, and I minded everybody and didn't vex em none. Us didn't go to church none, but I goes now to the New Prophet Church, and my favorite song is:

> Set down, set down, set down,
> Set down, set down,
> Set down, chil', set down,
> Soul so happy 'til I can't set down.
> Move the 'member, move Dan-u-el
> Move the 'member, move Dan-u-el
> Dan-u-el, 'member, don' move so slow
> Dan-u-el, 'member, don' move so slow
> Got on my rockin' shoes, Dan-u-el
> Got on my rockin' shoes, Dan-u-el
> Shoes gwine to rock me home
> Shoes gwine to rock me home, Dan-u-el
> Shoes gwine to rock me home, Dan-u-el
> Shoes gwine to rock me home, Dan-u-el
> Dan-u-el
> Shoes gwine to rock by faith
> Shoes gwine to rock by faith, Dan-u-el
> Shoes gwine to rock by faith, Dan-u-el

Move the 'member, move Dan-u-el
Move the 'member, move Dan-u-el
Got on my starry crown, Dan-u-el
Got on my starry crown, Dan-u-el.

They Called Us
McCullough's Free Niggers

Mandy McCullough Cosby
ANNISTON

My massa, Bryant McCullough, was a Chambers County man. He had so many slaves I can't tell you the number. He didn't know hisself how many he had. I is now ninety-five years old, and what I remembers mos' is the way the chillun roll aroun' in the big nurse's room.

Mist' McCullough raised niggahs to sell—and the little black chillun play round until bout sundown, they is give they supper. A long trough out in a cool place in the backyard is filled with good, cold buttermilk and cornbread crumbled in, and they each is give a spoon, and they eats they fill. Then they is ready for bed. Some of them jes fall over on the ground, asleep, and is picked up, and put on they pallet in the big chilluns' room. They was a old woman called the nurse, look after em. They get good care, for the massa 'pects they will bring good money.

Old Miss, she don't like to see them sold, and she cry every time, she so tender-hearted. But Mist' McCullough is jes like mens is today. He jes laugh and go on.

But he was good to his black folks. Folks called us "McCullough's free niggers." Wasn't much whippin' went on round our plantation, but on some places close to us, they whipped until blood ran down. Some places they even mixed salt and pepper in water and bathed em with it. The salt water'd heal, but when the pepper got in there, it burned like fire, and they'd as well get on to work quick, cause they can't be still.

One woman on a plantation not so far from us was expectin', and they tied her up under a hackberry tree, and whipped her until she died. Most any time at night if you go round that tree, you could hear that baby cry. I 'pect you could hear it yet.

Everybody said that was murder, and that something ought to be done about it, but nothin' ever was.

Mist' McCullough always give his folks plenty of somep'n to eat, and then he say, "I's lookin' for plenty of work." Niggahs fat and greasy can't do nothin' but work.

My mother was a loomer. She didn't do nothin' but weave. We all had reg'lar stints of spinnin' to do, when we come from the field. We set down an eat a good supper, and every night until ten o'clock we spin cuts of cotton, and reel the thread, and next day, the rolls is carded and packed in a basket to be wove.

Spinnin' wheels was in every cabin. There was so many of us to be took care of, it took lots of spinnin'.

She Can Just Remember
Her Husband's Name

Sara Colquitt
OPELIKA

Mr. Bill Slaughter and Miss Mary Slaughter was our master and mistress, and they had two chilluns, Marse Robert and Marse Brat. I had four brothers and sisters—Tate, Sam, Jennie, and Tenner. Us lived in log cabins with dirt floors, and they was built in two long rows. Us beds was nailed to the wall at one end and us used cornshucks and pine straw for mattresses.

Miss Mary was good to us, but us worked hard and late. I worked in the fields every day from 'fore daylight to almost plumb dark. I useta take my littlest baby with me. I'd tie it up to a tree limb to keep off the ants and bugs whilst I hoed and worked the furrow. All us niggers was fed from the big kitchen and wasn't hungry, but sometimes us would steal more food than was give us anyhow.

I was one of the spinners, too, and had to do six cuts to the reel at the time and do it at night plenty times. Us clothes was homespun osnaburgs, what us would dye, sometimes solid and sometimes checked.

'Sides working in the fields and spinning, sometimes I'd help with the cooking up at the Big House when the real cook was sick or had a passel of company. Us cooked on a great, big fireplace what had arms hanging out over the coals to hang pots on to boil. Then us had three-legged skillets what set right over the coals for frying and such-like. Us cooked sho'nuff bread in them days, ashcakes, the best you ever ate. They ain't nothing like these days.

"I was sold oncet before I left Virginia. Then I was brung down to Alabama and sold on the block for $1,000 to Mr. Sam Rainey, at Camp Hill, Alabama. I still worked in the fields, but I would cook for the white folks and help around the Big House on special 'casions. Our overseer was Mr. Green Ross, and he was a bad one, too. Mean, my goodness! He'd whup you in a minute. He'd put you in the buck, tie your feet, and then set out to whup you right.

He would get us slaves up 'fore day blowing on his big horn, and us would work 'til plumb dark. All the little niggers'd get up, too, and go up to the Big House to be fed from wooden bowls. Then they'd be called again for us to come from the fields and put to bed by dark. I useta stop by the springhouse to get the milk, and it was good cold, too, and tote it up to the Big House for dinner.

I had two chilluns, Lou and Eli, and they was took care of like the rest. Us useta have some good times. Us could have all the fun us wanted on Sat'day nights, and us sho' had it, cutting monkeyshines and dancing all night long sometimes. Some would pat and sing, "Keys not a-running, keys not a-running," and us sho' did more'n dance, I'm telling you. Sometimes, our mistress would come down early to watch us dance.

Next to our dances, the most fun was cornshucking. Marse would have the corn hauled up to the cribs and piled high as a house. Then he would invite the hands round to help shuck it. Us had two leaders or generals and choose up two sides. Then us see which side would win first, and holler, and sing. I disremembers the hollers jes now. My mind is sorter missing. Marsa would pass round a jug, too. Then they sho' could work, and that pile'd just vanish.

Us used the white folks' church in the mornin'. I joined the church then, cause I always tried to live right and with the Lord.

When the Yankees come through Dadeville, Alabama, us heard bout it, and Marsa hid his money and lots of fine things in the colored folks' houses. They never found em, neither.

I might nigh forgot who it was I did marry. Now, I knows. It was Prince Hodnett.

Homesick for Old Scenes

Clara Davis
MONROE COUNTY

I was born in the year 1845, white folks, on the Mosley plantation in Bellvy, jes north of Monroeville. Us had a might pretty place back there. Massa Mosely had near bout five hundred acres and most near to one hundred slaves.

Was Massa Mosely good to us? Lord, honey, how you talk. Course he was! He was the best white man in the land. Us had everything that we could hope to eat—turkey, chicken, beef, lamb, poke, vegetables, fruits, aigs, butter, milk—we jes had everything, white folks. Them was the good old days. How I longs to be back there with my old folks and a-playing with the chilluns down by the creek. 'Tain't nothin' like it today, nawsuh. When I tell you bout it you gwine to wish you was there, too.

White folks, you can have your automobiles, and paved streets, and electric lights. I don't want em. You can have the buses, and streetcars, and hot pavements, and high buildin' cause I aint got no use for em no way. But I'll tell you what I does want. I wants my old cotton bed, and the moonlight nights a-shining through the willow trees, and the cool grass under my feets as I runned round catchin' lightning bugs. I wants to hear the sound of the hounds in the woods after the possum, and the smell of fresh-mowed hay. I wants to feel the sway of the old wagon a-going down the red, dusty road, and listen to the wheels groanin' as they rolls along. I wants to sink my teeth into some of that good old ashcake, and smack the good old sorghum offen my mouth. White folks, I wants to see the boats a-passing up and down the Alabamy River, and hear the slaves a-singing at their work. I wants to see the dawn break over the black ridge, and the twilight settle over the place spreadin' a sort of orange hue over the place. I wants to walk the paths through the woods, and see the rabbits, and watch the birds, and listen to frogs at night. But they took me away from that a long time ago. 'Twarn't long before I married and had chilluns, but don't none of em 'tribute to my support now. One of em was killed in the big war with Germany, and the rest is all scattered out, eight of em. Now I jes live from hand to mouth, here one day, somewhere else the next. I guess we's all a-going to die iffen this 'pression don't let us alone. Maybe someday I'll git to go home. They tells me that when a person crosses that river, the Lawd gives him what he wants. I done told the Lawd I don't want nothin' much, only my home, white folks. I don't think that's too much to ax for. I suppose he'll send me back there. I been a-waiting for him to call.

Wed in the
White Folks' Parlor

Matilda Pugh Daniel
EUFAULA

Yassuh, white folks, I remembers lots of things that happen in the slavery times. I works around the house mistress, who was the daughter of Gen'l John Linguard Hunter befo' she married the massa. When I was a little pig-tailed nigger, I useta play round with Massa's chilluns. We play injuns in the woods, and build dams down on the creek, and swing in the yard, and sometime we sho' do devilish things. We hid red pepper in Old Black Bob's chewin' 'bacca, and you ought to seed the faces he made. It makes me laugh 'til yet. Then we tooken a skunk that us little white and black devils catched and turn him loose in the slave quarters. You ought to seed them niggers come a-flying outer there. They come out like a swarm of wet ants.

After I grew up, I married Joe Daniel, a house nigger, and Gen'l Hunter, the mistress's pappy 'formed the ceremony. We was married in the parlor, and I wore a party dress of Miss Sara's. It sho' was purty, made outer white tarleton [tarlatan—a thin, plain-weave, open-mesh cotton fabric finished with stiffening agents] with a pink bow in the front. I had a pink ribbon round my head, too, and Joe, he look proud of me. After the weddin' all the niggers on the plantation gathered about and we had a soiree in the backyard. Me and Joe moved to the quarter then, but I still worked in the house. Mistress warn't goin' to let nobody wash them julep glasses but me, and warn't nobody a-going to polish that silver but this here nigger, nawsuh.

Durin' the war us warn't bothered much, but after the Surrender, some po' white trash tried to make us take some land. Some of em come to the slave quarters, and talk to us. They say "Niggers, you is jes as good as the white folks. You is entitled to vote in the 'lections and to have money same as they," but most of us didn't pay no 'tention to em.

Then Massa James and Mistress moved to Washington, and Miss Sara wanted me to go with her to be her housemaid. She said she'd pay me money fo' it, but I couldn't leave my old man, Joe, cause he had a case of consumption. Joe died a year later and left me with four little chilluns. Us stayed round on the plantation, and the new massa paid us good money for workin', but soon the house catched fire and burn to the ground, and I have to move to Eufaula. I bought this little house with the money I saved. I has kinfolks in Detroit that sends me a little money, and some good peoples in Eufaula helps me out some, so I is in purty good financial shape. I ain't never 'sociated with no trashy niggers, and I ain't never intend to. I is goin' to be a proud and good nigger to the last.

Plantation Punishment

Carrie Davis

LEE COUNTY

Honey, there was a lot of cruel things done in slavery times.

Has you come to help me?

Them was good and bad times, Mistress, good and bad. I had a purty good marster, but the marster on the plantation that j'ined our'n was mighty mean. He was a bad man, no matter if the slaves behaved or not.

Honey, I 'members that he had regular days to whip all the slaves with straps. The straps had holes in em so that they raised big blisters. Then they took a handsaw, cut the blisters, and washed em in saltwater. Our old mistress has put salve on a heap of backs so they could git their shirts off. The shirts'd stick, you see. The slaves would come to our house for water, and Mistress would see em.

I was borned in Harris County, Georgia, and was bout ten or twelve when Freedom come. My mammy and pappy was Martha and Nathan Perry and had seven chillun. Besides me, there was Amy, Ida, Knoxie, Jim, Abraham, and Franklin.

Us lived in the Perry quarters. The cabins was made of split logs, put up edgeways, and daubed with mud inside and out. They was bout hundred yards from the Big House, where Marster Billy and Mistress Nancy lived. They was real good to us, too. Us ate at the Big House. Course the food was cooked on the fireplace, but us had meat, and greens, and biscuits. Us had collards and cabbage, too. Sometimes us would have wild game, because the men hunted lots and cotched rabbits, possums, and coons. They also cotched a lot of fish.

No'm, our beds warn't so good. They was homemade, and the sides was scantlings with legs nailed on. Then slats was nailed on top of it to put our shuck and straw mattresses on.

My grandparents was from Virginny. When I was a slave I was used as a house girl, and to help keep the yards clean and bring in water. Us wore mostly slips, wove in homemade looms, and they was osnaburg and homespun. We wore em Sunday and Monday the same. Us shoes was made at a tanyard, and they was brogans as hard as rocks.

I 'members that some of our white neighbors was poor

and didn't have no slaves. They would help us work. The overseer couldn't whip them, but he would make em work hard and late. I 'members, too, that the overseer waked us up with a trumpet.

They useta tell us that if us didn't work they was going to sell us to help feed the rest, and bless yo' soul, us niggers'd go to work, too. Marster wasn't mean. He would just lock the slaves in the crib for punishment. Ten slaves was sold. I seed many a nigger put on the block for five and six hundred dollars.

Us couldn't leave the plantation widout a pass, and you better not let em catch you with a book. Us walked to the white church and set in the back. Mr. Dawey Snell preach and baptize, and they had footwashings. Sometimes the niggers'd get so happy they would shout. They would keep shoutin' in the fields the next day and git a whipping.

If a nigger got out widout a pass, they set the hounds on you, and the patterollers'd tear you up, too, if you stayed out too late.

Us had such good times on Sat'day nights—frolic, dance, and cornshuckin's. Most of em would be drinkin', and sing, and holler:

Sheep's in the cotton patch;
Got em out Monday.
Had it been a white man;
Got em out Sunday.

Kid Kimbrough was our leader, and he could sing "Dixie," too.

Christmas mornin' us'd have a better breakfast, and they would give us rations at the Big House. When any of the slaves got married they went up to the white folks' house and jumped over the broom. That was the ceremony at the weddin'. And if Marster wanted to mix his stock of slaves with a strong stock on another plantation, they would do the mens and women just like horses. I 'members that when two niggers married, they got a big supper.

All us chilluns had a big time; played "Pretty Pauline," "Turn, Charlie," and such-lak.

When us got sick Mistress'd give horsemint, life-everlasting, goldenrod, and holly teas, yessum. And us wore asaforetida [asafetida] and popball seed.

When the Yankees come, they handcuffed our folks and took em off. Marster had his meat, corn, fodder, and such hauled in the swamp near the plantation. Them Yankees went as straight to it, as if they had seed us put it there. They burned it all up and took some niggers from the other farm.

When Freedom come, I 'members that Marster told us that us was free, but that we could stay on if we liked. Most of us stayed on with him for a spell. Now and then the Ku Klux Klan'd come around and beat on a nigger.

I married Charlie Gibson and had two chillun, twelve grandchilluns, and nine great-grandchilluns.

Honey, I's heard Abraham Lincoln's name, but don't know nothin' bout him. I got tired livin' among wicked peoples, and I wanted to be saved. That's why I joined the church and still tries to do right.

Wealth in the
Bodies and Souls of Men
Was Slipping Away

Louis Hughes
Tombigbee Salt Works

*Unlike the other narratives in this volume, this one by Louis
Hughes was not recorded by Federal Writers' Project interviewers, but rather was written by Hughes himself as part of a
memoir (Thirty Years a Slave: From Bondage to Freedom)
he published in 1897. It is included here because it reveals a
different aspect of slavery experiences in Alabama. Hughes was
a Mississippi slave hired out by his master during the Civil War
to work at a Confederate salt works in southwest Alabama.*

⁓

While I was absent on my last runaway trip, the Yankees had made a raid through Panola (Mississippi); and our

people had become greatly frightened. As soon as they had got back with me and my fellow runaways, they assembled a gang of slaves for the purpose of taking them to Atlanta, Georgia, to get them out of the reach of the Union soldiers. Among the slaves selected for the transfer were myself, my wife Matilda, and the seamstress. The others all belonged to Dr. Dandridge and Blanton McGee. Both the Drs. Dandridge went with us to Atlanta.

We traveled across the country until we came to Demopolis, Alabama, where we found Boss camped on the bank of the Tombigbee River with all the farm slaves from Bolivar County. This was the first time I had seen Boss since he was captured and taken to Helena. As my wife and I were the only ones in the gang who belonged to Boss, we left those with whom we had come and joined his gang. We all then went aboard a boat and were taken to the salt works, situated on the Tombigbee, ninety miles from Mobile. These salt works belonged to the rebel government. The first president of the works was Mr. Woolsey, of Salem, Alabama. During Mr. Woolsey's term, the first part of 1864, when we had been there some time, he wrote to Boss asking if he would sell myself and wife, and offering $3,000 for both of us. Boss was indignant at this and curtly refused. My wife acted as cook at the salt works, in the headquarters for the president, managers, and clerks. Mr. Woolsey was delighted with her cooking; her bread and rolls, he said, could not be surpassed.

When the election of officers of the works came off in the fall, Mr. Gallatin McGee was chosen president. Boss then hired us all, about 100 in number, to labor in these works, but he, of course, received all the revenue. The work assigned me was that of butler at headquarters, and my wife was cook. Both women and children, as well as men, were employed in these works. After some months labor here, soon after Gallatin McGee became president, Matilda and I were removed to the Montgomery headquarters, where we remained until nearly Christmas. A few days before that time, Boss came to Montgomery and arranged for us to meet him in Mobile. We started at the appointed time, reached the city in the morning, and I went directly to the hotel where he told me he would be. I found him at once, and he informed me all about his plans for the future, and what he expected to accomplish. He had purchased an island in the bay, a little way from Mobile, where he had decided to establish salt works of his own. All the brick and lumber for the buildings had been carried there, and work upon them was to be commenced immediately after Christmas. He intended to make a home for the family on the island; and, as soon as he could complete the works, to remove all his hands from the government works to his own. He was very enthusiastic over this scheme, claiming that he would make far more money by it than he was then receiving from hiring out his slaves. He told me that he would remain in Mobile two or three days and would go to Panola to spend the holidays, after which he intended to bring all the family to Mobile, and remain there until the island was in readiness to be occupied. There was to be a general break-up of the old home, and the beginning of a new manner of life.

I stayed in his room at the hotel all the forenoon, listening to his plans; then I went back where my wife was stopping. As I left his room, he said: "Lou," as he always called me, "I will see you and Matilda at the boat this evening." We went to the boat at the appointed time and saw the Boss, but he did not come near us. As the boat was about to put off, I looked and saw him walking up and down the levee, apparently much excited, running his hands nervously through his hair—a habit common to him when he was worried. He seemed greatly distressed. The military situation troubled him, for the Union army had conquered nearly everything; and the fact now stared him in the face that he would soon lose his slaves. He never dreamed in the beginning of the war that the Unionists would conquer, and that the slaves would be freed; but now he saw that not only all his wealth in the bodies and souls of men was slipping away from him, but that much, if not all, of the gain which these chattels had brought him was likely to "take wings and fly away."

We returned to the salt works the morning after leaving Mobile. Boss remained two days in Mobile, and then started for Panola, the home of his father-in-law; but, on his way, he was taken sick, having contracted a heavy cold which ran into pneumonia, and he lasted only a short time, dying on New Year's Day. He had taken cold in bringing the slaves from Bolivar over the river on barges. The river was overflowed about fifty miles out, and the only way he could get the slaves across was by using large barges made of logs. They were several days floating down in this way, before he could get out to the railroad at Jackson, Mississippi, where he transferred them to the cars. This was too much of an exposure and it killed him.

After Boss died all the plans were changed. Colonel Hunting, son-in-law of Old Master Jack, came down to the salt works and hired us all out there for another year. This was the beginning of the year 1865. Of master's plans concerning the island and his proposed salt works the family knew little, for they questioned me closely as to what he told me of the matter. What he spent on the island in lumber, brick, etc., was lost, as they knew nothing of the particulars of the expenditure. The madam remained at her father's, and the slaves at the works.

As I was here for another year, acting as butler, I thought I would try and see if I could not make some money for myself. I asked Mr. Brooks, the manager of the works, if he could get me some tobacco by sending to Mobile for it. He said he could; and on the fourth day thereafter, in the evening, it came. I was anxious to get it the same evening, but Mr. Brooks said: "Oh! I guess you had better wait until morning, then when you finish your work come down to the office and get it—you will then have more time to see the boys in the works."

In the morning I was up early, and after doing my morning work I was off to Brooks's office. When I went in he said: "There it is under the table." The package was so small I felt disappointed—a hundred dollars' worth ought to be more, said I to myself; but I took it, and went out among the men. I thought I would try to sell it at five dollars a plug, and if I could not sell it at that I would take four dollars. I must make something, for I had borrowed the money to buy it with; and I saw that to clear anything on it, I must at least get four dollars a plug. The money which I had borrowed was from three fellow servants who had been fortunate in earning some little time and had saved their money.

The first man I met in the works bought two plugs, at five dollars each; and after I had been there about an hour all was sold. So I went back with a light heart. Mr. Brooks said to me at dinner: "Well, how did you get along with your tobacco?"

"I did very well," I said, "the only trouble was I did not have enough. I sold it for $180."

"Well," said he, "if you did, you made more clear money than the works here. How much a plug did you sell it for?" at the same time drawing out his pencil and commencing to figure it up.

"I had thirty-six plugs," said I, "and I sold them for five dollars a plug."

Nothing more was said just then, but after dinner Brooks and two of the clerks went out on the veranda to smoke. When they were in a good way smoking, Brooks slipped into the dining room, and said: "Well, that was fine; you got five dollars a plug for the tobacco?"

"Oh, yes!" I said, "tobacco is scarce, and they were hungry for it; it went like hot cakes—the price was not questioned, I sold at once."

"What is the prospect for selling more?" he asked. "Will you sell it for half the profit if I furnish the tobacco?" I said, "yes." So he sent the same day for a box of tobacco—about five hundred plugs. When the tobacco came the box was sawed in two and one-half sent up to my room. I put some fellows out as agents to sell for me—Uncle Hudson, who took care of the horses and mules at the works; John at the hospital; William, head chopper, among the 100 men in the woods.

Each brought in from $40 to $50 every two or three days, and took another supply. Sometimes, when I had finished my work in the afternoon, I would get an old pony and go around through the neighborhood and sell four or five plugs. It was a mystery to the servants how I got the tobacco; but I did not let on that Brooks was backing me. In two weeks we had taken in $1,600, and I was happy as I could be.

Brooks was a fine fellow—a northerner by birth, and did just what he said he would. I received one-half of the money. Of course, this was all rebel money, but I was sharp, and bought up all the silver I could find. Just as we got on the other half of the box, Brooks received word that the Yankees were coming, and to send all the hands to their masters. I was glad that I had made some money, knowing that I would need it if I gained my freedom, which I now knew was quite probable, as the Union forces were gaining ground everywhere. But the message ended my money making, and I prepared to go home to Panola.

Mr. Brooks fixed the return papers so that my wife and I could leave the party of slaves at Demopolis, and go on thence to Panola by rail, to convey the news to madam that all hands were coming home; that the Yankees were expected to capture the salt works within a short time. At Jackson, some seven miles from the salt works, we were delayed overnight by reason of lack of facilities for crossing the Tombigbee River. The report that the Yankees were coming through had created a panic among the white people; and hundreds, fleeing from their homes, had gathered at the river, waiting and clamoring for an opportunity to cross. Though slaves were property, and valuable on that account, the whites seemed to think that their own lives were in danger, and to be protected first. They therefore took precedence of us.

In the morning about seven o'clock a steamer was seen coming at a distance; but it could not be discovered at once just what the character of it was. The whites became alarmed. Some said: "The Yankees are coming." Others said: "It is a gun boat—they will surely fire on us." But as the boat drew near the people saw that there was nothing to fear—it was only the regular passenger boat.

Besides the hundreds of people, there were scores of wagons, filled with household goods to go over, and the passage was slow and tedious. We finally got across and traveled as far as Demopolis, where Matilda and I left the other slaves, and took a train and went on to Panola. I delivered the papers to the madam from Brooks, which told her all the particulars concerning the break up at the salt works.

She sent wagons right away after the other slaves who were coming back on foot. They were not brought back to Panola; but were hired out to different farmers along the road home—some in Jackson, some in Granada and others in Panola town. These were all small towns in Mississippi.

My wife and I went to work at Old Master Jack's, I on the farm and my wife at her old duties in the house. We longed for freedom, but were content for the time with hoping and praying for the coming of the day when it should be realized. It was sad to see the changes that had come to the white folks. Sorrow had left its impress upon all and we felt it, notwithstanding all that we had suffered at their hands. Boss had willed the homestead in Memphis to Mrs. Farrington, and she was getting ready to take possession. He had borrowed a great amount of money from her when he bought the island at Mobile; and the rapid coming on of the end of the rebellion destroyed all prospect of the success of his salt works scheme, even before his death, and really rendered him bankrupt. Hence the transfer of the Memphis property to her was the only way he could make good what he owed her.

The madam now had no home, but was compelled to stay with her father, Old Master Jack. She was sadly changed—did not appear like the same person. Her troubles and sorrows had crushed her former cruel and haughty spirit. Her mother had died a few months before, and then her husband had followed, dying suddenly and away from home. Then much of her property had been lost, and social pleasures and distinction were gone forever. Who shall say that the wrongs done her poor, helpless slaves were not avenged in this life? The last I knew of her she was still at her father's.